# The Four-Minute Mile

The notion of 'barriers' and records are central to the world of sport. Objectives involving the breaking of records are especially found in 'racing sports' such as track and field athletics. Arguably the most significant record to be broken in the twentieth century was the four-minute mile. This was a major target and many attempts to break the barrier were made in the 1940s, notably in Sweden. The British runner Roger Bannister eventually broke it in 1954.

This collection of original essays seeks to explore, 'excavate' and explain the breaking of the four-minute mile by Roger Bannister. The essays provide the background to the record breaking run, the way Bannister was represented in both Britain and abroad, an analysis of his heroic stature, what the record 'meant' for Britain in the 1950s and why it was Roger Bannister and not one of his adversaries who ended up with the new world record. The chapters provide interpretative accounts rather than statistical tables and, drawing on an interdisciplinary and international array of authors, supply fresh thoughts on an historic event in twentieth century sport.

This book was previously published as a special issue of *Sport in History.*

**John Bale**, Keele University.

**P. David Howe**, Loughborough University.

Sport in the Global Society

General Editors: J.A. Mangan and Boria Majumdar

# The Four-Minute Mile

Historical and Cultural Interpretations of a Sporting Barrier

**Sport in the global society**
General Editors: J.A. Mangan and Boria Majumdar

The interest in sports studies around the world is growing and will continue to do so. This unique series combines aspects of the expanding study of *sport in the global society*, providing comprehensiveness and comparison under one editorial umbrella. It is particularly timely with studies in the aesthetic elements of sport proliferating in institutions of higher education.

Eric Hobsbawm once called sport one of the most significant practices of the late nineteenth century. Its significance was even more marked in the late twentieth century and will continue to grow in importance into the new millennium as the world develops into a 'global village' sharing the English language, technology and sport.

*Other Titles in the Series*

**Disreputable Pleasures**
Less Virtuous Victorians at Play
*Edited by Mike Huggins and J A Mangan*

**Muscular Christianity and the Colonial and Post-Colonial World**
*Edited by John J MacAloon*

**The Games Ethic and Imperialism**
Aspects of the Diffusion of an Ideal
*J A Mangan*

**Freeing the Female Body**
Inspirational Icons
*Edited by Fan Hong*

**Sporting Nationalisms**
Identity, Ethnicity, Immigration and Assimilation
*Edited by Mike Cronin and David Mayall*

**Running Cultures**
Racing in Time and Space
*John Bale*

**This Great Symbol**
Pierre de Coubertin and the Origins of the Modern Olympic Games
*John J MacAloon*

**Kenyan Running**
Movement Culture, Geography and Global Change
*John Bale and Joe Sang*

**Olympism: The Global Vision**
From Nationalism to Internationalism
*Edited by Boria Majumdar and Sandra Collins*

**Modern Sport : The Global Obsession**
Essays in Honour of J A Mangan
*Edited by Boria Majumdar and Fan Hong*

**Ethnicity, Sport, Identity**
Struggles for Status
*Edited by J A Mangan and Andrew Ritchie*

**Pleasure, Profit, Proselytism**
British Culture and Sport at Home and Abroad 1700–1914
*Edited by J A Mangan*

**Sport Tourism**
*Edited by Heather J Gibson*

**Barbarians, Gentlemen and Players**
A Sociological Study of the Development of Rugby Football
*Kenneth Sheard and Eric Dunning*

**Athleticism in the Victorian and Edwardian Public School**
The Emergence and Consolidation of an Educational Ideology
*J A Mangan*

**Women, Sport and Society in Modern China**
Holding up More than Half the Sky
*Dong Jinxia*

**Sites of Sport**
Space, Place and Experience
*Edited by John Bale and Patricia Vertinksy*

**The Commercialisation of Sport**
*Edited by Trevor Slack*

**Doping in Sport**
Global Ethical Issues
*Edited by Angela Schneider and Fan Hong*

**The Tour De France, 1903–2003**
A Century of Sporting Structures, Meanings and Values
*Edited by Hugh Dauncey and Geoff Hare*

# The Four-Minute Mile

## Historical and Cultural Interpretations of a Sporting Barrier

Edited by
John Bale and P. David Howe

Routledge
Taylor & Francis Group
LONDON AND NEW YORK

First published 2008 by Routledge
2 Park Square, Milton Park, Abingdon, Oxfordshire OX14 4RN

Simultaneously published in the USA and Canada
by Routledge
711 Third Avenue, New York, NY 10017

First issued in paperback 2015

*Routledge is an imprint of the Taylor & Francis Group, an informa business*



Typeset in Minion by Datapage International Ltd., Dublin, Ireland



*British Library Cataloguing in Publication Data*
A catalogue record for this book is available from the British Library

*Library of Congress Cataloging in Publication Data*

ISBN 13: 978-0-415-75948-9 (pbk)
ISBN 13: 978-0-415-40015-2 (hbk)

# Contents

# Series Editors' Foreword

*SPORT IN THE GLOBAL SOCIETY* was launched in the late nineties. It now has over one hundred volumes. Until recently an odd myopia characterised academia with regard to sport. The global *groves of academe* remained essentially Cartesian in inclination. They favoured a mind/body dichotomy: thus the study of ideas was acceptable; the study of sport was not. All that has now changed. Sport is now incorporated, intelligently, within debate about *inter alia* ideologies, power, stratification, mobility and inequality. The reason is simple. In the modern world sport is everywhere: it is as ubiquitous as war. E.J. Hobsbawm, the Marxist historian, once called it the one of the most significant of the new manifestations of late nineteenth century Europe. Today it is one of the most significant manifestations of the twenty-first century world. Such is its power, politically, culturally, economically, spiritually and aesthetically, that sport beckons the academic more persuasively than ever- to borrow, and refocus, an expression of the radical historian Peter Gay- 'to explore its familiar terrain and to wrest new interpretations from its inexhaustible materials'. As a subject for inquiry, it is replete, as he remarked of history, with profound 'questions unanswered and for that matter questions unasked'.

Sport seduces the teeming 'global village'; it is the new opiate of the masses; it is one of the great modern experiences; its attraction astonishes only the recluse; its appeal spans the globe. Without exaggeration, sport is a mirror in which nations, communities, men and women now see themselves. That reflection is sometimes bright, sometimes dark, sometimes distorted, sometimes magnified. This metaphorical mirror is a source of mass exhilaration and depression, security and insecurity, pride and humiliation, bonding and alienation. Sport, for many, has replaced religion as a source of emotional catharsis and spiritual passion, and for many, since it is among the earliest of memorable childhood experiences, it infiltrates memory, shapes enthusiasms, serves fantasies. To co-opt Gay again: it blends memory and desire.

Sport, in addition, can be a lens through which to scrutinise major themes in the political and social sciences: democracy and despotism and the great associated movements of socialism, fascism, communism and capitalism as well as political cohesion and confrontation, social reform and social stability.

The story of modern sport is the story of the modern world-in microcosm; a modern global tapestry permanently being woven. Furthermore, nationalist and imperialist, philosopher and politician, radical and conservative have all sought in sport a manifestation of national identity, status and superiority.

Finally, for countless millions sport is the personal pursuit of ambition, assertion, well-being and enjoyment.

For all the above reasons, sport demands the attention of the academic. *Sport in the Global Society* is a response.

J.A. Mangan
Boria Majumdar
Series Editors
Sport in the Global Society

# Introduction: The Sporting Barrier: Historical and Cultural Interpretations of the Four-Minute Mile

John Bale & P. David Howe

The year 2004 witnessed the 50th anniversary of what many regard as one of sport's most significant moments – the breaking by Roger Bannister of the 'four-minute mile'. Celebrations were held at Oxford's Iffley Road running track, where Gunder Hägg's record was broken on 6 May 1954. Several articles memorializing the event were found in the newspapers and a television film recorded the history of mile-running. Bannister's record remains firmly lodged in popular sporting histories and imaginations. It is also frequently referred to in academic works on sports history, the history of running and the sociology and cultural analysis of sport *per se*.

Bannister has been presented as the epitome of the British sporting hero. He has also been seen as a legacy of the past, a time in which the world of track and field athletics possessed only a passing resemblance to the sporting landscape of half a century later. The best athletic tracks today are made out of high-tech compounds, companies that make the shoes and clothing the athletes wear pay the top stars handsomely for endorsing their products. An international track and field star is a professional athlete. Bannister ran on cinder tracks and is regularly represented as the consummate amateur.

This collection of essays explores the historical and cultural significance of the first four-minute mile at a time the world mile record is less than 3 minutes 45 seconds. [1] Whether this detracts from the achievements of the key individuals involved in the pursuit of this barrier is one of the questions raised in this collection. Indeed, the manner in which contemporary records are achieved is not completely distinct from how Sir Roger Bannister achieved his greatest feat. Today, in the disciplines of the middle and long distances, both on the track and roads, athletes often of high calibre are paid handsomely for pacemaking (or 'rabbiting') races at world-record pace. This practice is commonplace throughout the world on the Grand Prix circuit, creating a marked distinction from the Olympics, World Championships and Commonwealth Games where such actions are 'illegal'. Authorities in charge of the sport once proud of its amateur roots have been pressured to recognize professionalism. The International Amateur Athletics Federation has recently changed its name to the International Association of Athletics Federations since it had long since lost the battle for the maintenance of amateur ideals.

It has been alleged that the slippery slope to professionalism was given a boost on the evening that Roger Bannister became the first man to run a mile in under four minutes. [2] Reflections on the destruction of the four-minute barrier have seldom been critical of either the staging of the event or the principal individuals involved. [3] It is the purpose of this issue to shed a critical light on the events surrounding the first four-minute mile and it is hoped that its readers will gain new insight from the historical and cultural interpretations of the breaking of this barrier which in 1954 was seen by some as on a par with the first ascent of Mount Everest.

Some observers have even contested the legitimacy of the four-minute mile. In 1954 it was considered almost illicit to have pacemakers in a race. It can even be argued that the four-minute mile event was not really a race at all. But the event did not officially contravene the rules and regulations of the 1950s as both Brasher and Chataway officially finished the race and there were others present in the field – but it was a race only in name. The event was staged with the use of pacemakers who were requested to run at a predetermined speed.

The use of pacemakers had been a common practice at Oxbridge and almost all of Bannister's best results were achieved by this highly rational approach. His years at Oxford produced steady athletic and academic progress. Before 1950 he had reached international class, and in that year, following the completion of his studies at Oxford, he came third in the European 800-metres championship. Two years later (by then an intern in a London teaching hospital) he had achieved a stunningly fast time-trial over three-quarters of a mile which his friend Norris McWhirter timed as a new world's best performance. His pacemaker was Chris Chataway, another Oxford man. Bannister was regarded by many as a favourite for the 1952 Olympic 1,500 metres in Helsinki, but he finished in fourth place, a result that met with considerable criticism from the British press.

As Britain entered 1953, the national mile record was held by the English athletic archetype Sydney Wooderson, whose time of 4 minutes 4.2 seconds was set in 1945 in Gothenburg. In May 1953 Bannister attacked this record at Oxford at the annual meeting of the Amateur Athletic Association (AAA) and Oxford University Athletic Club. With Chataway again the pacemaker, Bannister recorded a new British record of 4 minutes 3.6 seconds. A month or so later he bettered this time in unusual circumstances. A mile event was inserted into the Surrey Schools Championships, held at the London University track at Motspur Park. It was almost a 'secret' event and few press reporters were there to see it. Paced again, mainly by Chris Brasher, Bannister finished in 4 minutes 2 seconds. However, Brasher had jogged around the track at such a slow pace that he appeared ahead of Bannister on the final lap. Arguably, this was the most cynical approach to record-breaking yet seen, and the British Amateur Athletic Board refused to ratify it as a record.

These details flesh out some of the events leading up to 6 May 1954, the date of Bannister's world-record-breaking mile and, we might add, his 'unofficial' equalling of the world's 1,500 metres record. [4] We might add that the new world mile record set that day lasted only 46 days. It was improved by the Australian John Landy (3 minutes 57.9 seconds) who, at Turku in Finland, led from almost gun to tape. Could it be argued, therefore, that the first 'real' sub-four-minute mile was run by Landy? And could it be argued that this was a far greater achievement than Bannister's? The showdown between the two four-minute milers took place in the Empire Games in Vancouver, where Bannister beat his Australian adversary in a personal best time. This victory by Bannister was, perhaps, not surprising because the front-running Landy could be seen as his first legitimate pacemaker. Bannister followed that with another victory at the European Championships at Berne, where he easily won the 1,500 metres. And there his athletic career ended.

This clinical kind of statistical history will not be carried much further in the pages that follow. Instead, the authors seek to examine, interpret and explore the meaning and construction of the four-minute mile and its legacy. This is undertaken from an interdisciplinary perspective.

## The plan of this collection

The notion of the athletic record lies at the base of most of the articles collected here. The word 'record' is not immediately transparent and has been a somewhat controversial concept with which sports historians have grappled. The origins of record-making and record-keeping have been vigorously debated. [5] Since the nineteenth century questions have been raised about the tension between victory and athletic records. [6] It is also possible to recognize several kinds of records, and this question is addressed by Jim Parry in the opening chapter of this work. Parry basically sets the philosophical scene for the record. He suggests that there are several categories of record and suggests several factors that sustain an apparent fascination with the record performance.

The next five chapters focus mainly on the responses and the reactions to various representations of the four-minute mile, dealing with its coverage in the press, in books and on film. Bannister as an athlete and person – and his running tactics and the four-minute mile – have not been seriously analysed and contested. Roger Bannister himself, as well as cultural commentators and contemporaries reflecting upon the significance of the four-minute mile, have claimed that the achievement was welcomed by a British public ground down by the post-war years of austerity. The feat was also hailed as a statement of British quality, in rivalry with runners from the United States and Australia in particular. Roger Bannister was also presented as a national hero. In his article, Alan Tomlinson explores the context of austerity, and responses to the Bannister record in local press reports are evaluated as a way of exploring the premises of popular claims. The concept of the trope is employed to demonstrate how sporting actions and moments can be the vehicle for the expression and the perpetuation of social and cultural values which contribute to modern forms of myth-making.

The media coverage of Bannister's career during his athletic and post-athletic career was far from being free of controversy. Much of this controversy was fuelled by the press and in his article John Bale complements Tomlinson's chapter by examining the fractured nature of Bannister's representation in the broader national and international press. Bale also considers Bannister's place as a sporting hero, an appellation that has been frequently applied to him. It is shown, however, that the 'hero' is not only a slippery concept but also one that is geographically, socially and historically situated.

Bannister's image was, of course, represented globally, even in nations that used the metric system where the mile was rarely run and for whom it carried less status as an athletic event. Nevertheless, in the USA it was met with rapturous applause, though as Caroline Collins points out in her contribution, Bannister's image was placed alongside that of the US hero Wesley Santee who, with Landy, had for some time been a favourite to break the four-minute barrier. The relative significance of each of these athletes in the US press changed over time, adding a temporal dimension to heroic status. In particular Collins highlights recent revisionist writings of Santee that change his 1950s image of an aberrant athlete to that of an American hero.

Less well-known than the written texts about the four-minute mile 'business' are the filmic representations of the event. It is recorded that one of Bannister's friends, Norris McWhirter, [7] contacted the BBC to alert them to the possibility of a world record. A lone cameraman turned up and the result is a treasured record, albeit unrecognizable from the modern televisual representation of sport. Without McWhirter's foresight, however, the event would not have received the close scrutiny that the film provides and ensured the validity of the record. However, as Garry Whannel points out in his article, Bannister's 1954 performance took place during the formative period of television sport and by modern standards the BBC coverage was crude. More central to Whannel's chapter is his deconstruction of the BBC-Australian television film, *Four Minute Mile*. Whannel not only explores the similarities and differences between this, and other filmic drama-documentaries of British sport but also focuses on the mythical nature of the representation of Bannister.

Jim Denison takes a rather different tack in his contribution by examining the attitude of other four-minute milers to the very concept of the four-minute barrier. Having once been broken, it might be thought that the 'barrier' would no longer be recalled as such and become redundant as a mark of achievement. Denison suggests that this may not be the case and that many post-Bannister runners still see the four-minute mark as a significant target.

The next three contributions focus on training and performance. Arnd Krüger, basing his ideas on 'training theory' seeks to explain why it was Bannister and not one of his adversaries described earlier who was the first to break the four-minute obstacle. He attributes Bannister's success to a combination of 12 factors, all of which were in Bannister's favour. These ranged from Bannister's likely disposition towards caffeine consumption in the form of tea to his propensity to take to the mountains of Wales and Scotland, where the monotony of track training would be relieved. His article is followed by John Hoberman's enquiry into the place of Roger Bannister in the debate about amphetamine consumption in the 1950s and 1960s. Amphetamines (Benzedrine or 'pep pills') were widely available during Bannister's period as an athlete and medical doctor. Hoberman finds it astounding that Bannister claimed to know nothing about such practices until pressed by an American drugs expert in 1957. Hoberman does not go so far as to claim that Bannister was a consumer of such substances himself but raises the question about the four-minute miler's reticence about even discussing the subject. The final contribution to this collection is authored by P. David Howe and explores the 'science' of interval training in the 1950s. This method of training was specifically used by famous coaches of the era, notably Percy Wells Cerutty, the coach who influenced John Landy, and Franz Stampfl, who was heavily involved in Bannister's preparation for the 1954 athletic season.

Sports records, and even the four-minute mile in particular, remain subjects of interest for sports fans, sports scholars and researchers in other disciplines who see sport as a fruitful source of data for their own researches. [8] We hope that the contributions that follow will add to this interest and, at the same time, inform readers of the varied approaches that can be applied to sport in history.

## Notes

[1] The record for the mile at the time of writing is 3 minutes 43.13 seconds, by Morocco's Hicham El Guerrouj, set in 1999.

[2] See Chapter 14 of Pat Butcher, *The perfect distance – Ovett and Coe: The record breaking rivalry* (London, 2004).

[3] For more critical accounts surrounding this historical event, see this volume and John Bale, *Roger Bannister and the four-minute mile* (London, 2004).

[4] The result was 'unofficial' because it was recorded by a single timekeeper, Ross McWhirter.

[5] Allen Guttmann, *From ritual to record* (New York, 1978).

[6] For example Montague Shearman, *Athletics and football* (London, 1897).

[7] Norris and Ross McWhirter's first publishing enterprise was titled *Athletics World*. It was a monthly athletics magazine aimed at the aficionado more than the lay fan. It was initiated in 1953 and ceased publication in 1957.

[8] See, for example, Flavio Toxvaerd, 'Record breaking and temporal clustering', unpublished paper, available online at http://pluto.huji.ac.il/~toxvaerd/, accessed 7 November 2005.

# The Idea of the Record

Jim Parry

## Introduction

This paper examines the idea of the sports record and its relation to our ideas of excellence, achievement and progress. It begins by recovering and reviewing the work of Richard Mandell, whose definition of the record emphasizes three central ideas: statistic, athletic and recognition. It then considers the work of Henning Eichberg, Allen Guttmann and Mandell, [1] from the 1970s onwards, on the genesis of the modern sports record, explaining and developing their ideas via a distinction between descriptive and emulative records, and between different kinds of emulative records. This then permits an analysis of contemporary athletic and sports records. The idea of the 'significant record' will also be advanced, offering the four-minute mile as an example, alongside the breaking of the sound barrier and the ascent of Everest, in an attempt to explicate our continuing fascination with such exceptional achievements.

Since it has often been argued that the origins of our modern concern with records are rooted in the idea of modernity itself (rationalization, standardized conditions, ever more sophisticated means of quantification, the role of applied science and, more generally, of the scientific world-view), it then looks at the contribution of recent discussions of sport technologies and the logic of quantifiable progress, [2] considering the place and importance of relative emulation and of the qualitative evaluation of sporting performances.

Finally, in examining the ideas of excellence, progress and achievement, the paper will try to put 'our obsession with records' [3] in perspective, as but one way in which we respond to and evaluate sporting performance.

## The idea of the record

In his seminal paper 'The invention of the sports record', Mandell says that the 'idea of the record' is young. [4] 'The notion of the sports record is itself a refined product of a complex of ideas and practices unique to a democratic, industrial society.' [5] His initial definition of the record is that it is a 'generally acknowledged statistic indicating the unique nature of a supreme athletic performance of a recognized kind'. [6] Let us examine in turn the three central ideas of this definition: statistic, athletic and recognized.

### *1. A statistic – an abstract*

In Ancient Greek competition, for example, 'winners were always decided in proximate comparisons or contests; the victory was *over* someone else' and so 'the victor lived in history; his performances did not'. [7] In the eighteenth century, Englishmen, he says, began to race against time or distance, and so began the 'fascination for performance in the abstract', [8] made possible only through the existence of more finely calibrated instruments for the measurement of time or distance. Universal records then depended on the development of communications networks to assist the harmonization of standards and the emergence of democracy and equality of opportunity.

So ancient athletes ran in the present particular – their contests were against each other in the here and now – whereas modern athletes also run against the abstract, timeless standard that is the record.

*2. Athletic (not 'sporting') performance – sports records or athletic records?*

From pedestrianism (the walking and running feats and races of the eighteenth century), via the invention of the stopwatch, to the four-minute mile – the image at the forefront of the mind for authors such as Eichberg, Mandell and Guttmann in the 1970s seems to have been that of the individual runner – of the athlete, not the sportsman or the gymnast. [9] The nature of the athlete's interest in both the present and the abstract is produced by the kind of performance assessment possible – the actual performance being precisely measured and quantified in units.

By contrast, the footballer is not primarily interested in the statistics of the game, or the quantification of his or her team's performance. [10] Rather he or she is interested in the qualities of the performances of the individuals and of the team as a whole. Such an interest is conditioned by the fact that such qualities produce the result.

Of course, the actual result involves quantification to the minimal extent of goal-counting; and there may be a further interest in the relation of that actual result to the accumulation of points in a league, or to progress to the next round of a knockout competition. But this is quite different from athletic quantification, in which the athlete's actual performance is quantified.

Brownell acknowledges that, at least for Eichberg, the 'quintessential' modern sport was track and field athletics, which is a sport that lends itself to 'easy' measurement, standardization and comparison. [11] Its salience in the 'Eichberg/Guttmann/Mandel hypothesis' [12] is an indicator that the nature and importance of other sports, equally as modern, might have been overlooked in virtue of the 'nice fit' of athletics. For other modern sports retain other kinds of assessment or record-keeping than that identified by the hypothesis as the quintessentially modern record.

For example, the concern of footballers with 'world records' is minimal. Scarcely any meaningful ones exist, because of the very different contexts and conditions within which contests take place, and the very different qualities exhibited on different occasions. 'Abstract' achievements at the world level don't make much sense, apart from the primitive counting of national victories in the World Cup. And yet football is the world's most popular sport. Codified in England in 1863, it meets all Guttmann's criteria of modernity *except* for the obsession with records.

Not all sports keep world records, as the achievements in some events are too dependent on the layout of the course or venue, which may not be bounded by precise rules. Other sports or events do keep records, but do not regard them as particularly significant – for instance, marathon world records are regarded as far less important than on-track athletic events.

I think this shows that, whereas the origins and development of modern sports are indeed directly linked in many ways to the modernization and civilizing processes, the role and importance of quantification in those processes must be examined sport by sport. And the *kind* of quantification observable as important in some of the most popular world sports (e.g. standardization of playing areas, line markings, goals etc.) is not the kind important for its records. Whereas athletic records are typically universal, some other sports records are typically not. This is an important observation, given the role and importance of quantification in relation to the record in the Eichberg/Mandell/Guttmann hypothesis.

## The problem of recognition

Mandell notes that, while descriptive records have been with us through the ages, he finds the first use of 'record' in a sporting context in 1868, and he credits Montague Shearman as 'the first sports historian to use the term "record" alone with the assurance that his audience would know that he was referring to sports performances'. [13] To become a record, a performance has to be recognized by some competent authority. For example, now that we have established international federations in many sports, they are responsible for setting, maintaining and monitoring the conditions for record-setting.

Mandell further notes that, 'since they were invented by Anglo-Saxons in the late nineteenth century, records have continued to improve – this providing irrefutable evidence for the dynamic idea of progress'. [14] The point here is that such an idea of progress is dependent on the context it inhabits – and the context here is that of the competent authority that has the power to determine the conditions of recognition of a particular performance as a record.

Peter Radford, a former British Olympic sprinter, has recently described a number of eighteenth-century attempts to complete a sub-four-minute mile. [15] In his view, there is good evidence to suppose that 'professionals', running for wagers, were successful in their attempts, but that the Victorians who codified our sports were 'ideologically driven to exclude large parts of society' so as to eliminate 'unfair' competition from those who competed for money or whose jobs gave them advantages. For a while, two sets of records were kept, but then the earlier ones were forgotten and a new era of amateur athletics began.

The Amateur Athletic Association was able to determine the conditions of acceptance of an athlete, a performance, a venue and measuring instruments. Indeed, the earlier performances cannot be verified for accurate measurement of distance and time, a level track, the requisite conditions for a 'race' having been observed and so on – and they were done by professionals. Radford concludes:

> And so on 6 May 1954, almost exactly 184 years after James Parrott's first four-minute mile, Roger Bannister became the first amateur to run a mile in four minutes on a flat, level 440-yard track. It was an immense achievement. . . . It should not, however, overshadow the achievements of those pioneers who went before, men who dreamed of, and may well have achieved, the four-minute mile more than 150 years earlier, but who did it for money. [16]

If Radford is right, some pre-modern performances challenge those of the twenty-first century – which should lead us to wonder just how good those athletes of yore would have been if they had been assisted by modern technologies (footwear, other equipment, track materials and preparation, sport science applications, nutritional analysis, food supplementation – even doping).

The problem of recognition, then, may be partly to do with the *difficulty* of recognizing 'pre-modern' performances, because they were inadequately quantified or standardized. But it may also be to do with the *ideology* of recognition, according to which certain performances are excluded on social, political or moral grounds.

## The Eichberg/Guttmann/Mandell hypothesis

Let's back up a little and review: the Eichberg/Guttmann/Mandell hypothesis says that modern sports are different from the games, pastimes and sports played before the Industrial Revolution. Modern sports emerged along with industrial society, and both are characterized by an emphasis on achievement, rationalization and quantification, suggesting seven interrelated characteristics of modern sports: secularism, equality, bureaucratization, specialization, rationalization, quantification and (the obsession with) records. [17] This is not to say that pre-modern sports had none of these characteristics, or that all modern sports have them all – just that modern sports each involve a systematic interaction of some or all of them, and to a greater degree. For example, there is a dispute as to whether ancient sports were quantified. Did ancient Egyptian archers seek to shoot arrows through thicker metallic targets than each other? Did Greeks seek to surpass rivals by winning a series of events? Did medieval heralds keep score at tournaments?

The exchange of letters between Carter and Guttmann (both 1979) clarify what is at issue here. Carter asserts that 'surely medieval "athletes" kept records, even if only in their heads', and equates both 'lusting to unhorse' the opponent and 'the desire to outperform' him with 'breaking the record'. [18] Guttmann's response is that noting something down, seeking to out-perform the opponent or counting outcomes – none of these counts as even close to the modern conception of the record.

Kruger and Ito also dispute the claim that quantification of physical performance specifically characterizes and spreads from modern industrial society. Offering an account of the Japanese *chikaraishi* (rock-lifting competition), primarily from 1664 to the Meiji era, the authors claim a 'natural' desire to win and to quantify and record performances among various elements of the Japanese population; thus, they argue that the process of measuring and recording performance output was neither unique to nor entirely dependent upon Western culture, and may even be a cultural universal.

Here we must simply repeat a point previously made: the claim of the Eichberg/Guttmann/Mandell hypothesis is not that pre-modern sports had none of the characteristics they identify, nor that all modern sports have them all – just that modern sports each involve a systematic interaction of some or all of them, and to a greater degree. *Chikaraishi* may have elements of measuring and recording, but these elements are not integral parts of a structured world-view.

Guttmann's mature view is that the emergence of modern sport coheres with the spirit of the age, representing 'the slow development of an empirical, experimental, mathematical *Weltanschauung*', [19] and Eichberg emphasizes 'the process of rationalization and achievement orientation'. [20] Despite their theoretical differences, they agree that there is something different and special about modern sport, which such analyses seek to capture.

## Kinds of record

In the foregoing I have mentioned in passing several ways of noticing a sports record. Now we should attempt a conceptual review. We may begin by noting the distinction between descriptive and emulative records.

### *Descriptive records*

Early usage of the word 'record' referred to the 'attestation or testimony of a fact' that appeared 'noteworthy to a chronicler'. Key ideas captured here include:

- the preservation of some event or fact (which suggests some assessment of relative importance, or noteworthiness);
- the affirmation, confirmation or recognition of it as knowledge (which suggests some claim as to truth).

We see these ideas represented in common phrases such as:

- It is a matter of record;
- To go on the record;
- To keep to the record;
- As God is my record.

This usage is best illustrated in the legal context, where it means something like 'the fact of having been committed to writing as authentic evidence of a matter having legal importance'.

In the sports context, any data thought to be worth recording relating to any sports events worthy of note constitute sports records. It is in this sense that Cashman says:

> The records of an Olympic Games consist of archival files, books, reports, videos, photographs, art work, plans, memorabilia, and even internet sites: they constitute a valuable educational and cultural asset and resource. However, until recently, the value of records has not been fully appreciated. Records are the central component of legacy. [21]

We call these 'descriptive' records because they simply record data. [22] However, this does not mean that they are value-free or that they are unimportant. They have been thought to be noteworthy, whereas others have not. The concept of recognition has been especially important in establishing what does and does not count as worthy of record. Descriptive records also express the value of simple participation. For some participants, to have been recorded as present at an event, even if finishing last, is extremely significant. [23]

*Emulative records*

Whereas descriptive records simply recognize and keep a record of noteworthy facts or events (and all records are records in at least this sense), emulative records keep note of the best comparative performances in their category. However, there are three kinds of emulation. These are:

a. *Relative emulation*: that is, out-performing others in particular contests in the here and now (this game, this season, this competition – resulting in wins, placings etc);
b. *Absolute emulation*: that is, doing something that has not been done before (reaching the North Pole, breaking the sound barrier, or climbing Everest). However, this is tricky – for example, what are we to say about the second climbing of Everest? This is emulative (meaning that it equals or betters the first performance), or it may seek absolute emulation in climbing Everest by a different (more difficult) route, or under other conditions, such as in winter. There is clearly room for some dispute here, as people strive for the recognition of their achievements as noteworthy. One thing to notice, though, is that absolute emulation has been with us since pre-modern times, since circumnavigating the globe would also count.
c. *Universal emulation*: equalling or surpassing the best quantified performance in its category on record, across time and space, as kept by a properly constituted and accepted recognizing authority.

The central insight of the historians is that modern sport was created in the image of modern society, which produced the necessary conditions for the emergence of 'universal emulative' records. Without the standardization of conditions, the means for accurate measurement etc, there is no possibility for the kind of comparisons necessary for universal emulation.

In addition, we might distinguish between in-contest and accumulative records. *In-contest records* refer to the times, distances or scores in a particular competition or context. For example, in the (English) Football Association (FA) Challenge Cup competition the record score is Preston 26 Hyde United 0 (1886) – but this is for rounds proper, not the many qualifying rounds. In the context of the final, however, the record is Bury 6 Derby County 0 (1903).

*Accumulative records* refer to a series of performances in a particular competition or context (most FA Cup final wins or appearances, e.g. Lord Kinnaird's nine appearances and five winner's medals). They might also be called 'historical' records, or 'career' records.

The Eichberg/Guttmann/Mandell hypothesis argues that the origins of our modern concern with records are rooted in the idea of modernity itself. However, we are now in a position to note that it is only universal emulation that is specifically linked to modernity, while modern sporting records may take any of the above forms. They may simply note performances (e.g. give the results and other details of all fixtures for the season), or they may keep track of the best performances (in this race, this year, ever, in this country, Europe or the world, at this level, for men or women etc). Many of the most important records in our most important modern sports are not of the universal emulative kind. So it looks as though the 'modern' record has been overemphasized as characterizing modern sport.

Mandell, for one, sometimes writes as if modern sports records were all of the absolute emulative kind, whereas they are a mixture of the descriptive and of the three kinds of emulative. The truth in the Eichberg/Guttmann/Mandell hypothesis lies in its emphasis of the emergence of the universal emulative as the uniquely modern. And in this it is surely correct, since it is only modern conditions that permit the universal emulative. Nevertheless, we must insist that all kinds of records are with us and around us. Modern conditions do not push one way only.

## An example: football, the FA Cup and the Premier League

The descriptive records of the FA Cup are extensive, all scores having been recorded since the competition began in1871. [24] As we have noted, the record score in the FA Cup rounds proper is 26–0. But, when playing in some round of the FA Cup, teams are not trying to beat that score. Rather, they are simply trying to win *this* game *now* – to beat the other team, with a view to progressing to the next round – and 1–0 will suffice. [25] Thus, football matches are usually to be seen in terms of relative emulation.

However, sometimes the context is important. More than the immediate win may be at issue in the context of the competition of which the present game forms a part. To be sure, if I want simply to win the Cup Final, 1–0 will do. But consider the case where I want to win the league, and I need to win the last match against the league leaders by three clear goals to achieve equal points and a better goal difference than them and thus win the league. Here I need better than 1–0, but still I need only three more goals than them, and no more, to achieve my aim – that is to say, I still don't need to beat (or to have in mind) some record-winning performance.

Indeed, in football, record performances seem to be by-products of the activities of players and teams over time. There is some point in collecting and recalling data such as the highest number of appearances for a club, the highest-scoring total for a season or a career and so on. Some of these accumulative records may indeed be cherished as personal milestones or achievements. But they are not related to 'absolute' recognized achievement in the way that world athletics records are. In track and field, athletes compete relatively for victories, medals and championships, but they may also and simultaneously compete universally to hold a record. For the former, they must necessarily compete against the others in their particular and immediate contest – but for the latter they are competing against the abstracted performance of all athletes in all contests of the same kind.

## Another example: did the better team win?

In athletics, the best athlete on the day wins, barring injuries and excuses. But in football and other game-sports we can legitimately and interestingly ask whether the better team won, barring injuries and excuses. The very possibility of this question (the idea that the result is not everything) illustrates the difference between athletics and game-sports.

One way of bringing out this difference more clearly is by using Gilbert Ryle's distinction between task verbs and achievement verbs. Achievement verbs are 'episodic', meaning that the incidents they describe occur at a particular moment. An athlete can run for quite a while, but wins only in an instant. [26] The task of the race is to run, and the achievement is to win. It looks like we have two things here – but we don't. For the winning athlete, there is no second act after the running that constitutes the winning.

Running is his performance task, but in saying that he achieves a win we 'are asserting that some state of affairs exists over and above that which consists in the performance'. [27] It isn't that he *does* one thing (runs the race) and then he *does* one more thing (wins it). He wins *by* running. Just by the running. Achievements, says Ryle, 'are not acts . . . but . . . the fact that certain acts . . . have had certain results'. [28] Ryle was not the first to notice this. Paul says in I Corinthians 9:24: 'Know ye not that they which run in a race run all, but one receiveth the prize?'.

In football and other game-sports it is different, because the task/achievement descriptions are a bit more complicated. There are many different kinds of actions, from particular actions such as shooting/scoring to the most general such as playing/winning. The task is to play well, and the achievement is to win. But in game-sports it is quite possible to execute a task to the highest standard and still not be successful. Opponents can impede one's own performance, or counteract it, no matter how good it might be. Others in the team can under-perform, or team cohesion can fail even when individual performances are good. Then there is the role of luck or chance.

The task/achievement analysis shows that in athletic sports the aim, purpose or end cannot be specified independently of the manner of achieving it. For the athlete, his quantified result is constituted by his actual performance.

In game-sports, however, the aim, purpose or end *can* be specified independently of the manner of achieving it as long as it conforms to the limits set down by the rules or norms – for example, scoring a goal. For the footballer, the result is 'supervenient' on his performance, so that the qualities of his actual performance may or may not contribute to the production of the result. [29] In addition, we should notice the difference between individual and team sports. Obviously, in the former my performance constitutes the whole performance and I alone am responsible for it, whereas in the latter my own performance merely contributes to the whole performance and the players are jointly responsible.

These points have consequences for our view of what constitutes excellence in a sporting performance. In athletic sports, excellence is necessarily connected to winning, but in the case of game-sports, excellence may be exhibited which does not produce a win.

For excellence in game-sports may be characterized in terms of style or success – the 'better' team may lose. One team may do all the 'right' things, look 'good' for most of the game, dominate play and yet fail to score and be beaten by a late scrappy goal. The fact that the aim of the activity can be specified independently of the manner of achieving it means that claims to excellence are ambiguous. They could refer either to success in terms of victory or to quality of style or to both, and this raises the interesting question of the relationship between the two.

Let me explore this by way of an example from football. Since it isn't simply winning that always defines excellence in game-sports, we should not be surprised to encounter the following sort of dispute:

A thinks that X are a marvellous side to watch – an example of all that is best in football – even though they were nearly relegated last season.

He thinks that team Y, despite their consistent success, are not only a dull side, but also represent all those insidious influences which have destroyed English football both as a spectacle and as a serious claimant to European, let alone world, eminence.

B thinks that X present no threat to a well-organized and determined team, although when they 'click' they can play some very good football. He thinks that what makes Y the best team is simply that they win matches and competitions; that they seem to be able to win or draw even when they do not play particularly well.

A appeals to considerations of style, even though its manifestations are sporadic, whereas B appeals to the more objective measure of games and trophies won. I think that there is something to be said for both points of view, but that, as they stand, both are faulty.

B is right about winning. Since the point of playing football as a serious sport is to win points as a means to winning the championship or ending the season as high in the league table as possible, a team which consistently fails to do this cannot be one of the better ones. However, B might be taking a short-sighted view. Performance in this season's competition is not the be-all and end-all. If he is really concerned about winning and about Y's being able to win things not only now but in the future, and not only here but elsewhere in the world, he must also be concerned with the way in which winning the league influences the way in which his team plays. If current policies aimed at winning Premiership points result in the suffocation of reserve talent or the inability of individual players to cope with vastly differing situations, then winning now might be to sacrifice winning later.

A, however, is right to stress the importance of style. For, even though excellence of style will never guarantee victory, there must be some relationship between what counts as good style and the likelihood of success, and in addition to this, emphasis on style demonstrates a less parochial and short-term regard for winning.

While B simply wants Y to win, A wants X to exhibit good style, thinking that, in the long run, it will be better for X (in domestic and foreign competition) for his country and for football. It isn't enough to say that excellence is embodied in Y because they won the Premiership. But, against A, it must be said that criteria of 'good style' can only be developed by reflecting on those qualities which are likely to bring success. If X consistently fail to succeed, we must re-examine the claim that they exhibit good style.

Excellence in game-sports, then, has to do not only with winning, but also with the way in which winning is achieved.

## Records and excellence

As we have seen, it has often been argued that the origins of our modern concern with records are rooted in the idea of modernity itself (rationalization, standardized conditions, ever more sophisticated means of quantification, the role of applied science and, more generally, of the scientific world-view). But this does not mean that our concern with excellence is limited to our concern with records – for there are different kinds of excellence.

I believe that we can apply the concept of excellence to the whole range of achievement, since we can distinguish the following conceptions:

a. absolute excellence, achieved only by those who reach standards higher than all others;
b. distributional excellence, achieved by all those who reach standards previously reached only by some;
c. relative excellence, achieved by all those who reach standards higher than some others;
d. personal excellence, achieved by all those who reach standards higher than their previous best.

It is (a) that all advocates of excellence seem to be after, above all and eventually; (b) may either be seen as instrumental to (a) or not really very important; (c) may be regarded by some as hardly a case of excellence at all and (d) may or may not be also (a), (b) or (c).

My own view is that excellence is not simply a concern of those who have already achieved or expect to achieve the dizzy heights – it is (and should be) the concern of us all. Excellence does not just extend to absolute excellence, which may simply amount to a relatively few isolated individuals, admired by the rest of us for their ability and dedication, winning trophies and setting records. It extends also to the wider distribution of higher standards of achievement, thus widening the base and raising overall quality.

And it also extends to as many people who find it worthwhile to achieve something themselves, for then their *concern* for standards, whatever the absolute status of their own achievements, will provide the context and support for those who are able to achieve what the rest of us cannot achieve. As Gardner says,

> we cannot have islands of excellence in a sea of indifference to standards . . . those who achieve excellence will be few at best. . . . But many more can achieve it than now do. Many, many more can try to

> achieve it than do now. And the society is bettered not only by those who achieve it but by those who are trying. [30]

That is to say, society is bettered by absolute excellence, but also by a better *distribution* of excellences, and also by the *concern* for and *appreciation* of absolute excellence which is likely to follow.

I believe that the educative and coaching task is not simply to promote absolute excellence, but also to promote that broad base of understanding and concern for standards and achievement in which all kinds of excellence can flourish. In this regard it is perhaps worth pointing out that the Olympic motto *citius*, *altius*, *fortius* means 'faster, higher, stronger' (and not 'fastest, highest, strongest'), indicating a commitment not just to absolute excellence, but to other kinds of excellence, too.

## The logic of quantifiable progress and the limits of human performance

What, then, is the place and importance of relative emulation and of the qualitative evaluation of sporting performances? Loland points out the logical difference between activities such as athletics and football. The former are governed by the logic of quantifiable progress, whose values include measurement, standardization, objectivity, specialization and record-setting. [31] The latter, including the great team games of the world, are governed by the logic of qualitative progress, whose values are quite different. Here, points won and goals scored are not precisely quantified, nor quite so tightly related to a measured quality of performance. (I score one goal, and only one, no matter how excellent or lucky the strike.) Standardization (that all pitches and conditions be as nearly as possible exactly the same) is foregone in favour of equality of opportunity (that the conditions on the day be the same for both teams). Instead of particular and specialized abilities, these activities require learned skills and techniques and interaction with others, and present an opponent who has the opportunity to frustrate one's best efforts – all contributing to a focus on the particular qualities of *this* match, here and now.

Those who consider the logic of quantifiable progress to be at the heart of modern sport – the idea that 'record sport' is the quintessentially modern kind of sport – commit themselves to a view of sport that is vulnerable to what Loland calls 'the impossible demand for unlimited progress within limited systems'. [32] That is to say, the internal logic of record sport carries the seeds of its own destruction, since the demand for unlimited quantitative progress comes up against the finite limits of human performance.

This is a grave limitation, and also spawns moral dangers, since the ceaseless quest for records is fed by over-training, fanaticism, doping and cheating. It also promotes excessive technologization, overemphasizing the role of science in augmenting human performance and in expanding our perceptions of human limits – altering the conditions of performance (tartan tracks, glass-fibre poles), personal equipment (shoes, clothing), training regimes, recovery times, nutrition and so on.

As Brownell says, Eichberg calls modern sport 'the ritual of records', a kind of dehumanizing treadmill, contrasting it with the kind of sport that exists within the 'culture of laughter'. [33] Loland's comparable conclusion is that we have a duty to cultivate the 'joy' of sports by maximizing qualitative progress, because this is what makes sport most meaningful to us as human beings. Basic physical qualities such as strength, speed and endurance are seen not as ends in themselves, but as only a means to qualitative goods, which are based on techniques, tactics and practice. The logic of qualitative progress offers the possibility of 'unlimited growth in unlimited systems', which have the capacity for the endless provision and satisfaction of the joys of sport. [34]

## The significant record

Finally, we should note that some records are of more significance than others. They are remarked upon not just because they are noteworthy, but because they are exceptionally so – they come to be seen for some reason in some way (perhaps somewhat arbitrarily) as exceptionally significant markers.

To be a record, a performance has to be recognized by some competent authority. For example, now that we have established international federations in many sports, they are responsible for setting, maintaining and monitoring the conditions for record-setting. Before that, however, there was no such mechanism. Even in athletics, established world records are, surprisingly to some, less than a hundred years old: 'After the Olympic Games in Stockholm in 1912, . . . the International Amateur Athletic Federation officially declared all the results obtained by the winners as the first world records'. [35]

To be a significant record, however, it has to be recognized more widely in society, to take on a kind of noteworthiness that exceeds its meaning within its immediate context, to capture the imagination of the people. [36] This requires something greater than relative emulation, so we are in the realm of the absolute and/or the universal. One such target was the four-minute mile, but why did it assume such significance?

One kind of answer is to be found in the social significance of the ideas of excellence, achievement and progress in the post-war optimism of the 1950s. Was the ascent of Everest humanly possible? Could a manned aircraft break the sound barrier without breaking itself into pieces? Would the mile ever be run in under four minutes? It is difficult now to appreciate the extent to which these were real questions for people at the time – it genuinely seemed to many that these things were impossible, perhaps dangerously so. One is reminded of the critics of rail travel in the nineteenth century who genuinely feared that, if humans travelled through the air much faster than a horse could run, their breath would be snatched away and they would suffocate.

It is similarly difficult, now that they have been done, to appreciate the significance of those achievements at the time. People marvelled at the rapidity of progress and the apparently ever-increasing standards of excellence, as a string of the most significant human achievements followed each other in a period of less than ten years, from the breaking of the sound barrier in 1947 to the first satellite to orbit the earth in 1957.

Another kind of answer is to be found in the uniqueness of a certain performance in its class. Of course, all emulative records are unique when set, but significant records are unique even among the emulative records in their class. For example, the world air speed (or land speed) record may be broken continually, but the one time when the sound barrier was broken was unique in its class. It constituted a kind of milestone, or landmark.

Yet another kind of answer is to be found in the fortuitousness of convention, and how our attention is drawn to some focus. The four-minute mile was and remains a significant record, but part of its attraction lies in the conventions of measurement that describe it. Four laps, four minutes, one mile – a kind of perfectly described task that sets it apart from equally significant performances that could not be so symmetrically described.

For example, there is no metric equivalent: while for Bannister 3.59.4 dips under 4.00, no one ever got so excited about the two-minute 30-second kilometre, or the three-minute 40-second 1500 metres, neither of which quite has the same ring to it as the four-minute mile. Or, again, no one much noticed the women's five-minute mile. [37] Doubtless there is a gender issue here, but the one-minute lap also has an appeal lost to the one-minute 15-second lap.

Maybe these three factors – the socially produced focus on excellence, the landmark achievement and the serendipitous description – go some way towards illuminating our continuing fascination with the various kinds of exceptional performance. Whether or not it is the definitive marker of modern sport, the record is here to stay.

## Notes

[1] Henning Eichberg, 'Recording and quantifying is not natural', *Stadion*, 4 (1) (1977), pp. 253–6, Allen Guttmann, *From ritual to record* (New York, 1978); Richard Mandell, 'The invention of the sports record', *Stadion*, 3 (2) (1976), pp. 250–64.

[2] See especially Sigmund Loland, 'The logic of progress and the art of moderation in competitive sports', in T. Tännsjö and C. Tambuurini, eds., *Values in sport* (London, 2000).

[3] Allen Guttmann, *A whole new ball game* (Chapel Hill, NC, 1998), p. 6.

[4] Mandell, 'The invention of the sports record'.

[5] Ibid, p. 250.

[6] Ibid.

[7] Ibid, pp. 251–2. See also M. Golden, *Sport and society in ancient Greece* (Cambridge, 1998), pp. 61–2.

[8] Ibid, p. 255.

[9] Here I use the idea of 'athletics' as used in British (but not American) English. In Britain, 'athletics' is usually taken to mean track and field events, whereas in America the term has wider application.

[10] Again I use the British meaning, to distinguish football from American football, in which quantification is required both for game progression and for the assessment of player performance.

[11] Susan Brownell, 'Thinking dangerously', in Henning Eichberg, *Body cultures* (John Bale and Chris Philo, eds.) (London, 1998), pp. 22–44.

[12] John M Carter and Arnd Krüger, eds., *Ritual and record: Sports records and quantification in pre-modern societies* (New York, 1990), p. 1.

[13] Mandell, 'The invention of the sports record', p. 259.

[14] Ibid, p. 260.

[15] Peter Radford, 'The time a land forgot', *The Observer*, 2 May 2004.

[16] Ibid. Note here, in passing, that Derek Ibbotson was the first modern man to run a mile in four minutes (4:00.0 'exactly'). Bannister was the first to do it in under four minutes.

[17] Guttmann, *From ritual to record*; Brownell, 'Thinking dangerously'.

[18] J.M. Carter and A. Guttmann, 'Letters to the editor', *Journal of Sports History*, 6 (2) (1979), pp. 87–90.

[19] Allen Guttmann, 'From ritual to record: A retrospective critique', *Journal of Sports History*, 28 (2) (2001), p. 7.

[20] Eichberg, *Body cultures*.

[21] R. Cashman, 'Olympic scholars and Olympic records: Access and management of the records of an Olympic Games', *Fifth International Symposium for Olympic Research* (2000), p. 207.

[22] There is a further descriptive use of the term 'record' which we might mention, even though it is not relevant to us here: the idea of a trace, or series of marks or remains, made or discovered in a medium. This usage includes, for example, written records, archaeological evidence, 'the fossil record' or a 'gramophone record'.

[23] See the example of George Dole, who finished sixth and last in the Bannister mile: S. Turnbull, '"I didn't know Roger had broken four minutes. Then I heard the Tannoy . . ." – the Bannister anniversary', *The Independent*, 2 May 2004.

[24] This is not quite true. All results in the FA Cup have been recorded since 1871, but some of the actual scores have been lost, e.g. in 1871–2 and 1873–4, when three ties are recorded as draws, with no scores, and 1883–4, when all scores for the second round are absent: G. Green, *The official history of the FA Cup* (London, 1949), pp. 182, 194.

[25] Of course, this itself is rule-dependent. Not always has a win been a necessary condition of progress to the next round. In 1871 Crystal Palace and Hitchin drew 0–0 in the first round of the first FA Challenge Cup competition, but both proceeded to the next round to play other teams. This was in accordance with Rule 8 of the competition: 'In the case of a drawn match the Clubs shall be drawn in the next ties or shall compete again, at the discretion of the Committee.' The same procedure was followed in the progress of The Wanderers and Crystal Palace, who drew in the third round, into the semi-final. In fact, The Wanderers played only two games in four rounds, winning only one of them, in order to reach the final, which they won. Two games were 'walk-overs' (see Green, *The official history,* pp. 11, 182).

[26] G. Ryle, *The concept of mind* (London, 1963), p. 143.

[27] Ibid.

[28] Ibid, p. 144.

[29] This way of characterizing the distinction was suggested to me by the distinction between purposive and aesthetic sports made in another context by David Best, 'The aesthetic in sport', *Journal of Human Movement Studies*, 1 (1) (1975), p. 43.

[30] J.W. Gardner, *Excellence* (New York, 1961), p. 133.

[31] Loland, 'The logic of progress', pp. 40–4.

[32] Ibid.

[33] Brownell, 'Thinking dangerously', p. 30.

[34] Loland, 'The logic of progress', p. 48.

[35] I. Balas-Soeter, 'Limits to competitive sport', *Proceedings of the International Olympic Academy*, 9th session (1969), pp. 215–59.

[36] Bannister, *The first four minutes*, 50th Anniversary Edition (Stroud, Gloucs, 2004) p. 157.

[37] J. Stuart, '50 years ago, Roger Bannister became a sporting legend . . . Why is his female equivalent just seen as an also-ran?', *The Independent*, 20 April 2004.

# Bannister's Feat in Austere Times: The Construction and Reproduction of a Sporting Trope

Alan Tomlinson

## Introduction: Massaging the myth

In his chapter on the institutionalization of modern sports in Great Britain, Allen Guttmann makes mention of the 'resurgence' of athletic glory in the late 1970s and the early 1980s when Sebastian Coe and Steve Ovett battled for records and medals in middle-distance running. He concludes his subsection on athletics, though, with an encomium to Roger Bannister:

> [T]he archetypal English track-and-field star was Roger Bannister, the slender, self-trained Oxford medical student who ran the first

> sub-four-minute mile. His record of 3:59.4, set on May 6 1954, was quickly broken, but Bannister survives as an anachronistic symbol of fair play. 'No athlete', he wrote in his autobiography, 'is content to take a prize accruing from a rival's misfortune'. Oxford, they say, is the home of lost causes. [1]

As John Bale has so clearly shown (see, especially, the following article in this issue) Bannister was not an Oxford student, and was certainly not uncoached, when accomplishing his legendary feat. That a scholar of such rigour and repute as Guttmann can continue to cultivate such misunderstandings of the nature and context of the Bannister moment is testimony to the partial and misleading way in which that moment has been interpreted in popular consciousness and a nostalgic collective memory, media representations of the history of British athletics and general academic syntheses themselves. Even where the essential modernity of the accomplishment is recognized, in Richard Holt's recognition of the 'sub-four-minute mile' as 'a superbly planned and executed achievement', Bannister is described as 'a medical student at the University'. [2]

One of Roger Bannister's pacemakers and training partners, Christopher Chataway, asking himself why the moment of Bannister's four-minute mile has endured, captured the sense of the end of an era:

> Why has the magic of this particular race worn so well? . . . We had just one good season and a couple of good races.
>
> But it is remembered . . . because it is seen now as the last flowering of amateurism. It was our lifestyle that enchanted the watching world. They fell in love with the idea that running was just a part of our lives. We were the last flickering of the illusion that world athletics might still be dominated by young undergraduates from Oxford and Cambridge. [3]

In this chapter I ask what kind of a world was actually watching as Bannister, aware that his great rivals, Australian John Landy and American Wes Santee, were close to running at or under the four-minute mark, orchestrated his early-evening run on home ground to achieve legendary status in the athletic pantheon. Passing through Los Angeles airport, Chataway recalls, he bought a book called *1,000 years and 1,000 people*, which purported to rank the men and women who 'shaped the millennium':

> These are the thousand most important people in the past 1,000 years. It lists St Thomas Aquinas, Charles Darwin, Winston Churchill. John Kennedy doesn't get in and Ronald Reagan doesn't make it – but Roger Bannister does. It's supposed to evaluate how famous a person

> is: what is his or her legacy to posterity, how they changed history and influenced the millennium. And there is Roger Bannister at 963 – towards the end admittedly, but none the less he's there. Isn't that wonderful? There he is with William the Conqueror and all the great old lags from the history books. Somehow what happened that day has passed into legend and into the language. [4]

Chataway illustrated his final point by recalling a cricket commentator hail the first 100-mile-an-hour delivery, by a Pakistan bowler, as 'the four-minute mile of cricket'. [5] In this way, Bannister's most famous race has acquired the potency of myth, in the classical sense of supernatural tales that reinforce a culture and its values. The more that is written of such myths based upon lived deeds and individual biographies, the more they are re-presented as cultural tropes rather than historical documentary. Bale has shown how Bannister's autobiography mixes scientific and romantic modes of writing and presentation, a curious blend of the rational and the aesthetic, but also reminds us that 'The sanitized space of the running track, devoid of serious competitors and manned only by assistants, replicated the laboratory. The four-minute mile was an experiment, a model to be empirically tested. Most of Bannister's key performances were not competitions; rather, they were scientific tests.' [6] In this reading, Chataway's explanation of the appeal of Bannister's achievement is incomplete, overemphasizing the idealist amateurism of the athletic culture and underestimating the thoroughly modern mode of preparation and execution that made the achievement possible.

Bale's analysis is not shared by all commentators. Bascomb's glowing tribute to Bannister and his rivals perpetuates the view that Bannister was 'an amateur who trained little more than an hour a day and for whom running was nothing more than a passionate hobby', a hero who 'achieved greatness on a cinder track he had helped build, in front of a small crowd, a handful of journalists, and a lone camera crew that had to be persuaded to attend'. [7] One participant in the Iffley Road race, witnessed by that small crowd, was American Oxford graduate student George F. Dole, documented by some as fifth in the race, with the spent Christopher Brasher listed as sixth. Dole reflects on the race:

> I realised immediately after the end of the race that I had been part of an historic occasion. There had been much debate as to whether the four-minute mile was physiologically possible. There had been a sort of 'sound-barrier' mentality . . . Roger Bannister's four-minute mile gave Britain as a whole a major boost. Recovery from the batterings of war was by no means complete and the United States

> had vaulted into a position of World Leadership. The coronation in 1953, and then Hillary's conquest of Everest and Bannister's mile, coming in quick succession, all had a touch of the glories of Empire and were something to be proud of in times that were otherwise rather dreary. [8]

The meaning and significance of the Bannister mile vary according to the witnesses brought to bear. How could the Revd Dole, a Yale graduate studying Hebrew as a postgraduate at Oxford, in 'equal parts competitor and spectator', as he recalled, in the race, [9] know what 'Britain as a whole' felt? Is it feasible to claim that the 'dreary' times of post-war Britain could be countered by athletic achievements, a version of the bread and races (or circuses) argument?

Sporting achievements and contests as popular cultural forms cannot be reconstructed in any definitive fashion. Raymond Williams, tackling the basic methodological questions of how to conduct critical cultural analysis in historical contexts, distinguished between three levels of analysis: the lived culture 'of a particular time and place', the recorded culture, and that which connects the first and the third levels, the 'culture of the selective tradition'. [10] No one can grasp the whole of the lived culture, but the researcher must be aware of its potential range, and be ready to expand the parameters of any framework for understanding a particular culture and its context. The recorded or documented culture can reveal much about the lived culture but, depending upon the scale of the analysis, may be understood only partially by the analyst. Successive analyses and interpretations contribute to a selective process by which cultural forms and practices come to be analysed, understood and known.

Sporting moments, then, must be understood as cultural constructions, replete with meanings, significant for how they express complex and at times contested values. They provide clues as to the ideological make-up of a particular culture and time. Acts or feats, moments or names, can constitute and act as a trope, in the classical definitional sense of the term: 'a figure of speech which consists in the use of a word or phrase in a sense other than that which is proper to it'. [11] William Gladstone, in his writings on classical Greek literature, wrote of the need to 'treat as a poetical trope this idea of kings as god-born or god-reared'. [12] Tropes, then, can perpetuate interpretations, contribute to myth. Looking at how the Bannister feat has been reported, recollected and recalled, is to engage in the study of a powerful trope.

## Reporting and recollecting the sporting moment

*The Times* reported the Iffley Road race in its news, not sport, section. The report was sandwiched between two reports on international affairs: one concerning some robust questioning of prime minister Sir Winston Churchill on the British position in relation to issues in Indo-China and US foreign policy; the other related to Geneva-based diplomatic meetings on the 'Viet Nam' question. Immediately below the Bannister report was a brief item announcing that Len Hutton would captain England in its forthcoming Test Match against Pakistan. As well as the report, extracted and summarized below, the paper included, alongside letters to the editor on a variety of topics, an overview of the mile – times and runners over the years – from the perspective of 200 years of the history of athletics (this is cited in the final section of this article). It also referred to the full match results of the Oxford match, available on page 3 of the paper, in the specific 'Sporting News' section:

> **4-Minute Mile – Triumph of R.G.Bannister – Poor Conditions Overcome**
> R.G. Bannister accomplished at Oxford yesterday what a whole world of milers had recently been bracing themselves to achieve first – the four-minute mile. He did so in conditions which were far from promising, and he did better than even time, for he finished weary but triumphant and mobbed by an encircling crowd, in 3min. 59.4sec. – three fifths of a second less than the magic four minutes. On the way, at 1,500 metres he had equalled another world record, shared by Gunder Haegg, the previous holder of the world record of 4min. 1.4sec. over the mile, Lennart Strand, another Swede, and Walther [*sic*] Lueg, of Germany. [13]

In the second paragraph, the context of the race – an annual athletics match between Oxford University and the Amateur Athletic Association (AAA) – was described, and it was noted that this was 'rather forgotten in the general excitement', with the small crowd making up 'for lack of numbers by an intelligent enthusiasm which enabled many among them to realize when the last lap was being run and Bannister raced well ahead, that something big was about to be recorded by the time-keeper – almost certainly a world record – perhaps the four-minute mile itself'. [14] The report's third paragraph was dedicated to a weather report – would the meeting go on at all? Would the showers of rain threaten the schedule? Would the 'strong gusty wind' scuttle the Bannister hopes? – and a summary of the results of other races. The fourth paragraph got to the core of the business, though, reminding readers that four of the six runners, including Bannister and his two pacemakers Brasher and Chataway, were competing for the three As, with just two university runners in the line-up. A short fifth paragraph described the first half (and a little more) of the race with Brasher – 'always a gallant and willing runner' – in the lead. The sixth and seventh paragraphs, subheaded 'A decisive phase', told how Brasher 'dropped back . . . he had deserved well of all concerned' and Bannister 'lengthened his magnificent stride' on the way to victory, 50 yards ahead of Chataway, who finished in his own personal best time of 4 min. 7.2 seconds. Spectators invaded the track and field: 'There was a sense of the wildest excitement – and what miserable spectators they would have been if they had not waved their programmes, shouted, even jumped in the air a little.' [15]

There had been miserable onlookers from afar, if not spectators, two years before when Bannister's disappointing fourth place in the 1,500 metres race at the 1952 Helsinki Olympic Games led him to review his performance strategies. Chataway recalls receiving a letter from Bannister, asking him to assist him in more systematic and rigorous training schedules. [16] In the year after the Helsinki disappointment, Bannister targeted the four-minute barrier. His achievement the following year created a British sporting great whose profile demands inclusion in any retrospective overview of the sporting times of post-war Britain. For Jonathan Rice, the year of Queen Elizabeth's coronation the year after her succession to the British throne was portrayed as a time of 'post-war greyness', when working people in particular viewed life with a mixture of 'hope and despair'. [17] Post-war rationing, New Year floods, an unstable international situation characterized by the Korean War and an intensifying cold war, dramatic criminal trials and executions – Rice paints a picture of early 1950s Britain that is barely recognizable as the same place as the affluent consumer society and culture that was opening up a decade later. For solace, in such a context, he goes on, people could turn to sport: 'In this grey and sometimes frightening world, people found that one way of forgetting the dreariness of their everyday lives was through sport'. [18]

Rice notes that such a form of escape and forgetfulness was a very domestic phenomenon at this time: the football FA Cup final (in 1953, the Matthews final when Stanley Matthews at last finished on the winning side in the competition), the Grand National steeplechase, international rugby tournaments (including France), Wimbledon and the golf Open Championship (even though dominated by the Americans) and cricket. In August 1953, at London's Oval, the England cricket team regained the Ashes in its series against Australia, after a gap of more than 20 years, having last triumphed on tour in Australia. England had last won the Ashes in England in 1926. The most prominent sporting moment of 1953 in even more international terms was, of course, Sir Edmund Hillary and Sherpa Tenzing Norgay's ascent of Everest on 29 May – a New Zealander and Nepalese, but members of a party led by Englishman Sir John Hunt. Looking for other great sporting moments of 1953, Rice dedicates a chapter to Roger Bannister, focusing upon the Motspur Park mile in which Christopher Brasher acted as his main pacemaker as Bannister set a personal best and national record of four minutes and two seconds, and the British Amateur Athletic Board refused to accept the record as 'it was not done in a bona fide competition according to the rules'. [19] Rice presents this as a pivotal moment on the way to 6 May 1954, when Bannister

> could not have achieved his goal without the pacemaking of two of his henchmen of 1953, Chris Brasher and Chris Chataway. As Chataway remembers it, they had learnt their lesson in dealing with officialdom. After the record had been broken and Bannister was gasping for breath as a vast horde of well-wishers slapped him on the back, Brasher and Chataway were asked by BAAB officials whether or not they were trying to win the race. Both replied, 'Yes. Of course.' The Motspur Park Mile had not been run entirely in vain. [20]

*The Times*'s 'small crowd' has become, in Rice's coffee-table portrait of the coronation year's sporting culture, a 'vast horde'. In 2004, BBC Television's feature *The First Four Minutes* showed more restraint and historical integrity than Rice, in its reconstruction of the race at Iffley Road. [21] The crowd was indeed small, and the well-wishers were clearly the friends and fellow athletes within the Oxford and Cambridge University athletic elites. The feature centres around a commentary by Bannister himself, and interviews with key players such as Norris McWhirter, former Oxford athlete and a sports journalist in 1954, and Christopher Chataway. The music of Elgar provides the background music at key moments, Bannister reads (as accompaniment to sepia images of a small boy running on a deserted beach) from the most aesthetically focused passages of his autobiography, [22] McWhirter smiles at the recollection of Bannister's achievement in the most British of distances, 'our' distance, the 'Imperial mile'. Chataway hails that memorable May day as 'the last hurrah of amateurism'. The BBC portrayal captures the sense of a privileged English elite taking on the world of ruthless modernity – the hard-training East Europeans, the win-at-all-costs Americans. And against all of this the programme points to the greyness of life in early 1950s Britain. But what was the reality of everyday life in post-war Britain? It is impossible to understand the cultural significance of the four-minute mile without considering that context at a little more length.

## The post-war years: everyday austerity, sport and leisure

Bannister has made much of the notion that the austere conditions of everyday life in post-war Britain made people ready for the excitement of sporting possibilities. There was still rationing, he has recalled; travel allowances restricted personal mobility and for many there was 'nothing to make up for having won the war, to make the peace worthwhile' [23] On the actual anniversary day of his race, Bannister reiterated this view, recalling the persisting austerity of the early to mid 1950s, and a sense of nagging financial crisis in the nation. People were ready, he said, for something 'to lighten the gloom'. [24]

The early 1950s were unrecognizable, culturally, from the later 1950s. Sissons and French, writing initially less than a decade on from Bannister's famed moment, remind us of the act of interpretative empathy that must be made to understand a culture characterized by the Labour Chancellor Sir Stafford Cripps's stress on the need for 'austerity' in the post-Second World War years:

> In the growing prosperity of the fifties there was perhaps a conscious turning away from memories of the days of rationing and shortages. And in many ways the atmosphere of the post-war years is incredibly remote. It is difficult to recall a time when so much idealism was in the air . . . when TV was only a metropolitan toy, ball-point pens a source of wonder, and long-playing records a transatlantic rumour. [25]

Shortage of material goods was a major feature of the period, and rationing of food and luxuries lasted into 1954. It was not just bacon, poultry and eggs that were restricted to the consumer and doled out according to your allocation of ration coupons; in 1946, 'the first concern of the new British international cross-country team was to find the 1,816 clothing coupons needed for all their shorts, vests and track suits'. [26] Cooper points out perceptively that for wartime children the post-war years, as rationing eased, were 'a revelation':

> They were lit by surprises: between 1945 and 1951 we saw not only the first pineapples and bananas of our lives, but the first washing-machine, the first fountain, the first television set. The world opening

> before us was not a pale imitation of one we had lost, but a lucky dip of extraordinary things we had never seen before. [27]

There were, though, well-established leisure practices in the everyday culture of the populace. In the late 1940s, record numbers flocked to Britain's cinemas (20 million loyal screen fans a week throughout the 1940s and into the 1950s) and its football grounds, creating what James Walvin has called a 'communal fizz' in the everyday and familiar culture of the time. [28] *Manchester Guardian* journalist Norman Shrapnel looked at the north-east Lancashire town of Burnley during its annual summer wakes weeks in 1951: '"Having a lovely time but glad to be back" postcards are being written, and all those kippers so tenderly dispatched,' he concluded his piece, entitled 'Burnley Sits Back'. [29] We meet Mr Briggs who is off on holiday 'away from home' – where else but to Blackpool? – for the first time since before the 1914–18 war. We glimpse the absurdities of the mix of the consumerist modern and the traditionally functional, as an 'elderly woman passes, pushing a very modern perambulator full of football boots'. [30] One young woman is '"off for my first taste of the blue Mediterranean"', sounding to Shrapnel 'brightly self-conscious like a radio script'. [31] Men on the tops of buses tell 'of a Burnley woman who went to America "just for a short holiday" fifty years ago, and has just flown home'. [32] There is an absence of the dramatic or the theatrical in these observations, and a sense of reassuring familiarities amidst cultural changes.

For those who remain in the town during the wakes weeks, the exotic arrives: 'The fairground population moves in, filling an entire side-street with great baroque caravans and disused omnibuses with tall zinc chimneys and clothes hanging to dry on the bumper bars.' [33] Burnley is

> looking gay, with almost Parisian touches of grace and imagination like the flower-baskets decorating the lamp standards or the elaborate plot near the bus-station with handsome plants spelling out 'Alderman Maxfield'. Summer hats are in full bloom, though a little the worse for the weather, like cottage gardens after a storm. [34]

While the townspeople of Burnley were holidaying in Blackpool or dressing for summer, in the capital almost eight and a half million were flocking to the South Bank, eight million to the Pleasure Gardens at Battersea, the latter having usurped the position of the Whit Monday Fair at Hampstead, North London, in the holiday calendar. These numbers made the Festival of Britain, described by Herbert Morrison, Lord President of the Council in the ailing Labour Government, as 'the people giving themselves a pat on the back', [35] an undoubted success. Gerald Barry, former editor of the *News Chronicle*, had urged Sir Stafford Cripps, when the latter was President of the Board of Trade, to consider a celebration of the mid-point of the century, and of the centenary of the Victorian Great Exhibition. Barry became director-general of the festival project, and announced the rationale behind the project to the national press, in October 1948:

> We envisage this as the people's show. . . . [1951 will be a year of] fun, fantasy and colour . . . [a year of] the fun and games which the bitter circumstance of the last few years have denied us . . . [a year in which] we can, while soberly surveying our great past and our promising future, for once let ourselves go. [36]

Modern designs and displays, technological novelties – the Festival of Britain was an initiative designed to make a modern statement, to bring colour, glamour and excitement into people's lives. As Michael Frayn put it, after 'five years of war, and a disillusioning peace which had brought nothing but continuing austerity, continued restrictions, and the threat of war again, the nation craved a brilliant holiday as some sort of tangible reward for its labours and sufferings'. [37]

Shortages were not just material, as Sissons and French have noted: 'A shortage of talent was also apparent in the world of sport, on which, with life drab and restricted in other respects, the public focused so much attention.' [38] Brian Glanville, looking mainly at the weakness of British football when playing abroad, and also at boxing and athletics, talked of 'six years of illusions' in a British sporting culture living on past reputations and borrowed time. [39]

Communal institutions in leisure might include the sports club, but this would be expressive of local status, the divisions of social class and the gendered dynamics of patriarchy; post-war austerity was hardly a recipe for cross-class integration and progressive gender politics. Sport, apart from a glance at the newspapers' sport sections and pages, merited no mention in the survey of English life and leisure produced by Rowntree and Seebohm in the late 1940s and published in 1951. [40] How, then, a few years on, would the local cultures respond to the Bannister achievement? Behind the national news story and the cinematic newsreel, what did the breaking of the four-minute mile mean to the people of Britain? To portray some of these responses, in the following section the local press responses in the two ancient university cities, and in selected small-town contexts in north-west England, are considered.

## Local receptions

### *Oxford: claiming the glory and telling the technical tale*

In Oxford, Bannister's run was genuine local news, reported in both the weekly *Oxford Times* and the daily *Oxford Mail*. [41] The former appeared on the Friday, the day after the race, and carried a back-page (page 16) story on it, alongside marriage announcements and accounts of local crime and other miscellaneous local items. It was a relatively small item, tucked in the top right-hand corner, comprising a short text and the famous photograph of Bannister crossing the finishing line. The headline was 'Bannister runs mile under 4 minutes – all records broken'.

The daily *Oxford Mail* had no coverage on the day of the race itself, the six o'clock evening timing of the run being too late to make the final edition of the paper. On the Friday, though, the front page was dominated by the story, which took centre position and occupied a whole quarter page. The *Mail* had its own reporter and photographer at Iffley Road, and the front-page coverage reflected this, comprising three story themes and five large photographs. The front page included only one other substantial report, on Labour politician Aneurin Bevan's driving charges (he had failed to stop his car at the scene of a collision). The photographs included exclusive shots of Bannister at different points throughout the race and at the end. The main story, substantial in both content and length (around 1,000 words) was an informed account of the race, citing the coach Franz Stampfl's words to Bannister: 'Try it,' Stampfl was reported as saying to Bannister, adding a spice of tension and drama to the story, it being a 'last-minute decision' that led to Bannister's success. This main theme in the report combined the technical detail with the tension of the moment. Bannister was quoted as being proud to have achieved the feat for his country, stating that he was pleased that this had been done by an Englishman. Two other shorter themes looked at the personal aspect ('Telegrams arrive – 1 a minute'), and described the busy day that Bannister's parents were now having, as well as confirming that there should – according to the athletics authority Jack Crump – be no problem ratifying the record. The second shorter story returned to the technical theme: 'Broke record on track rebuilt on his own idea'. Here we see something of the supportive infrastructure that Bannister had established for himself over the previous eight years, a whole redesign of the track to accommodate four laps for the mile. The *Mail* report was technically informed and revealing. On the back page, under the headline 'Bannister acclaimed', two small photographs showed Bannister at his hospital base in

St Mary's, Paddington (London) and holding telegrams. In its Saturday edition, the *Mail* carried a cartoon of Bannister on page three, made up of images of gramophone records, with names of record athletic times on the records, and all the records broken in half: Bannister the record-breaker, in the age of a new mass communications industry.

## *Burnley: finding the local link*

In the *Burnley Express and News* on the Saturday following the event, much was made of Bannister's link with the area:

> All North-East Lancashire is proud of 25-year-old Roger Bannister, the first man in the world to run a mile in under four minutes. Roger really belongs to this part of the country although he was born in Harrow.
>
> His father, Mr Ralph Bannister, is a Trawden man and lived in the village until moving to Harrow on his marriage. His mother, formerly Miss Alice Duckworth, came from Barrowford and is the daughter of Mr Robison Duckworth, a prominent cotton manufacturer there.
>
> DELIGHTED
>
> Yesterday [writes a *Burnley Express* reporter] I spoke to Roger's cousin, Mrs Harold Crowther, formerly Miss Mavis Bannister, of Higham Road, Huntroyde Padiham, whose husband, well known throughout the cotton industry, is a past president of Burnley Chamber of Commerce and connected with the National Chamber.
>
> 'We are delighted with this achievement' she said, 'the more so because Roger is just now sitting his finals in medicine.'
>
> Roger has a great deal of affection for Lancashire, not only because his parents came from the county, but because he loves the area and its people. 'The last time he was here was six and a half years ago when he was groomsman at the wedding of my son David, at St Luke's Brierfield,' added Mrs Crowther, 'and when he was leaving for home he told me he had had a thoroughly happy time.'
>
> In July Roger goes to British Columbia to run in the British Empire Games at Vancouver. An Oxford University graduate, Roger is now at St Mary's Hospital, Paddington, completing his medical studies. [42]

Here it is the theme of celebrity that dominates, and the report says more about the status of the people of north-east Lancashire than about Bannister or the news event. There are even inconsistencies in the report, as Bannister's cousin Mavis refers to him 'sitting his finals' when in fact he is in his hospital year and his university finals are well behind him. One wonders too, even for a busy medical trainee and international runner, how more than six years could pass without him expressing more directly his love for the area and the people. This is a typical 'angle' story, clinging on to the cloak of the new celebrity.

## *Cambridge: wider and narrower contexts and concerns*

The Friday night final edition of the *Cambridge Daily News* acknowledged the Bannister run in its column 'Sports Gossip . . . By the Looker-On'. The column's lead story was a football story: Cambridge City FC was accepted as a full member of the Football Association after five years as an associate member. The following story, 'Victory for O.P.s', told of Old Perownians' cricketing victory over Trinity College – a dramatic result, given that the eventual victors had been 9 runs for 4 wickets before rallying to 73 all out, and then dismissing Trinity for a mere 53 runs. The Bannister report – 'Bannister Takes It Easy' – was a single sentence: 'While Roger Bannister, the first man to break the 4-minute mile barrier was enjoying a little extra sleep in London today, his parents in Harrow were kept busy receiving congratulations on his amazing achievement.' This passing acknowledgement was followed by a report on the varsity game against the county cricket side Sussex. [43] In the earlier 'late special' edition the cricket match had not been reported, and the athletic landmark had received more column inches than either the local football club or the cricket match account. That version of the story had taken up in some detail the theme of the family, and national and international responses to the Bannister feat:

> After seeing his brilliant run in the extraordinary time of three minutes 59.4 seconds on Oxford University's Iffley Road track last night they [Bannister's parents] returned home, leaving their 6ft 24-year-old son, a medical student at St Mary's Hospital, London, to enjoy a quiet celebration with friends.
>
> Switchboard operators at the hospital, too, had to cope with a rush of calls from well-wishers in many parts of the country, all eager to offer praise to the man who has made history by his world record-breaking run.
>
> It is expected that the feat will be put forward soon for ratification by the International Athletic Federation.
>
> Mr Jack Crump, secretary of the British Amateur Athletic Board, has already received the necessary form giving full details of the race.
>
> 'It is perfectly in order,' he said, 'and there should not be the slightest trouble in obtaining ratification. It will be submitted to the Board's Records Committee, who will then send it forward to the International Federation. Bannister has done a great thing for British athletics. We are all delighted with his wonderful performance.

> I always thought that he could do it, and I am glad that he became the first to achieve it.'
>
> Dean Cromwell, who coached the 1948 US Olympics team, declared in Los Angeles, reports A.P., that Bannister's time was a 'great performance' but would be broken.
>
> 'Wes Santee can do it any day under favourable circumstances. What is to keep John Landy, of Australia, and Ingvar Eriksson, of Sweden, from doing likewise?'
>
> A.P. also reports that a New York Times editorial said today that Roger Bannister's mile win was 'an achievement the whole world cheers and thrills to, even in an age when the jet airplane can travel at 1,000 miles an hour.
>
> 'We may say "Well run" to Bannister, and congratulations to the British for bringing this record back home again.' [44]

This is a comprehensive report, assembled from the national dailies and the AP (Associated Press) wire services. It combines the human interest – proud parents and hospital colleagues receive the plaudits and protect the privacy of the athletic hero and instant celebrity – and the official acclamation: Jack Crump, suspicious of the tactics and practices of Bannister and his helpers, whose board condemned the Motspur Park Mile of 1953, sees no problems with this run. The report then locates the story in the international setting, pushing towards the theme of restoration of British pride on an international stage dominated by American Olympic might. The Iffley Road race was not enough of a story, though, to make a front page dominated by bigger international themes.

The lead stories on the front page were: the US's policy switch on Indo-China; a French cabinet meeting on Far East/Vietnam reverses; the sale and purchase by the government of Belgian rifles; Labour politician Aneurin Bevan's driving charges; US plans to build more atomic submarines; British and West German prospects for economic prosperity; a new minimum stipend for Church of Scotland ministers; the improving health of the Duchess of Gloucester; the anticipated warmer weather; the visit of Queen Juliana of the Netherlands to London; the conviction of an ex-detective for kidnapping; and the theft of silverware from a racehorse owner's home in Chalfont St Giles. The front page comprised the rather more serious themes of international relations, economic policy, crime and the weather. The Bannister legend merited not a mention on the lead page.

Many readers had other, more urgent things on their minds than the four-minute barrier. In the paper's 'Mainly for Women' section, for instance, 'the big food news' in the 'week-end food' subsection was the 'de-rationing of butter, cheese, margarine and cooking fats, after 14 years of rationing'. [45] Meat and bacon were still rationed, but there was plenty of pork about, some beef and mutton allocated to butchers too. But there 'is no lamb and no offal'. [46] The female readers could look ahead to a break, though, and the 'thinking ahead to holidays' subsection featured some one-piece swimming costumes, highlighting knitted ones 'blended with elastic yarn to fit as trimly as a second skin'. [47] So, early in the day Cambridge gave Bannister respectful space, but as the day wore on the local sports results took over: and, in the order of things, the seriously international news themes and the everyday concerns of living and getting by were of greater import than the athletic heroics in Oxford. Of course, one can speculate as to how this order might have been disrupted more noticeably should Bannister have been a Cambridge graduate, following in the footsteps of Cambridge athletic greats such as Harold Abrahams and Lord Burghley. But the news agenda in Cambridge on that early summer weekend of 1954 showed a local culture's concerns to be subsistence not spectacle, making do in a threatening and austere world.

### *Colne: the primacy of the local*

Back in north-east Lancashire a few months later, in the New Year of 1955, the *Colne Times* reviewed the previous year. [48] May 1954 was recalled for school exhibitions, drama society productions, the birthdays of long-lived local citizens, the appointment of local worthies, the death of a Rotarian, the crowning of the anniversary queen of the Methodist church, an outing of the Colne Blind Society supported by the Colne Darts League and the retirement of a local sportsman: 'After 21 years of loyal service, Colne Cricket Club's loyal wicket-keeper, Ellis Dickinson, a popular figure on all Lancashire League grounds, decided to retire from the game in May.' [49] Of course, this is a local overview, providing what local people want in an identity-affirming fashion. But even back in May Bannister could not displace the primacy of the local, or of the local consumption of the international cinema product. The day after Bannister broke the famous barrier, Alan Ladd, Jean Arthur and van Heflin, stars of the Western movie *Shane*, showing at the Savoy, dominated the front-page advertisements of the *Colne Times*; or you could go for the Warnercolor of *The Miracle of Fatima* at the Hippodrome. All the sports news inside the paper reported local matches and competitions, featuring in the main cricket, football and bowls, and with some mention of sailing and potholing. Running was not a prominent player in the local sporting scene.

## Conclusion: Beyond Juvenal – the spectacular and the mundane

The Roman satirist Juvenal observed how some forms of sport might symbolize the decline of a political spirit:

> Long ago, the people cast off its worries,
> when we stopped selling our votes. A body that used to confer
> commands, legions, rods and everything else, has now
> narrowed its scope, and is eager and anxious for two things only:
> bread and races.
> 'I hear that a lot are going to die'.
> 'No question about it. The kitchen is sure to be hot'. [50]

The motif of austerity and diversion from austerity, so widely posited by many to explain the appeal of sport at times of deprivation, political apathy or disillusion, implies that there is little else available to people, and that an event of high national profile will capture the imagination of the general population. National papers, cinematic newsreels, new broadcasting technologies – all of these can capture the excitement and thrill of the moment. But they do not tell all of the story.

Bannister's was not the only athletic culture of the post-war years. Boys' comics celebrated the working-class male who could compete against the odds, the fish-and-chip-eating tough of the track Alf Tupper. [51] In the Iffley Road race, behind the pacemaker Chris Chataway, Tom Hulatt of Tibshelf (Derbyshire) finished an honourable third place. Hulatt was running for the AAA in the event, arrived by train, by all accounts, and took a bus to the Iffley Road track. He was the only non-Oxbridge man among the six runners, brought in to give some credence to the claim that this was a race in an athletics meet or match. He died in 1990 and his obituary in a local paper, the *Chad*, recalled his place in athletics history: 'At the time Tom was a miner at Williamthorpe Colliery, and he would walk the five miles to work, move some 20 tons of coal with a shovel, then run the five miles home.' [52] Unthanked at the event, the lone representative from the race at the post-match dinner as Bannister and his friends were whisked to London for broadcast appearances and elite club hospitality, Hulatt would later mutter, with no malice but some sense of injustice, that the race was 'a set-up job', that he felt 'done', deceived. [53]

The athletics correspondent of *The Times* had, no doubt, had his copy ready for some time when Bannister gave him the chance to top and tail his piece 'Stepping-stones to the Four Minute Mile – Story of a Great Endeavour':

> The fascination of the round figure which conveys to everyone a sense of real achievement no doubt is one of the reasons why the four-minute mile has captured the popular imagination and spurred runners all over the world to what must seem to them, at the time at any rate, a supreme effort. . . .
>
> So the matter of the four-minute mile rested up to last evening. Bannister's performance, if formally ratified, will earn for him athletic immortality no matter how soon someone else goes a fraction of a second better – or even a shade better than that. [54]

Jack Crump, accepting the race as a valid one in terms of records, could write the following year that 'athletics must remain amateur because it cannot afford to become professional' [55] unless it became dependent on the morally dubious support of betting. Crump was flying the flag for an amateur-based athletics culture in decline, a sport that, after abysmal showings at both the 1948 London Olympics and the 1952 Helsinki games, gained a massive boost from Bannister. But as Brian Glanville has stated, writing about the post-war years, 'athletics – until Olympic year – is no more than a minor sport, watched and supported by the few'. [56] But if the few includes the privileged elites of the educated and upper classes, regularly covered by the most influential organs of the media, their achievements will be magnified, celebrated, commemorated and placed at the heart of the selective tradition. Within two days of his run, Bannister could read in *The Times* that, while 'the hero himself was resting quietly in London yesterday the athletics world continued to ring out its congratulations' on his 'great achievement', which was already producing 'echoes' around the world. [57]

No matter what 'revisionist view' [58] swathes of critical scholarship might foster, the Bannister trope survives impact. No matter what the indifference to the event of many elements in the local lived culture of the time, the four-minute mile motif remains the stuff of myth. Bannister is not mythical in the sense of historical fictitious figures from the past. He is of course very much a real – and 52 years after the race, a live – figure. But Philip Carter argues that 'common to all types' of mythical figures 'are names and deeds that have generated popular perceptions, or misconceptions, of British history' and that 'common to all is the power afforded to a generic cause' such as 'national rivalry . . . when expressed and interpreted through the medium of biography'. [59] The Bannister name and deed can in this sense be understood as myth. Therefore, no matter what lack of evidence there is to support Bannister's, and others', claims that his running was a spectacular diversion from austere times, their reading will be sustained.

There are multiple readings of any momentous cultural moment. The ascent of Everest has been a focus for intense debate between historians, showing how, in Gordon Stewart's words, 'an apparently autonomous event' can be 'rich in historical significance', and 'a great signal sender in British culture'. [60] The ways in which the 50th anniversary of Bannister's run was commemorated in the media and in publishing show how such signal-sending can work, how a selective tradition can, in spite of documentary evidence and the fullness of a wider lived culture, be reaffirmed. The selective interpretative tradition underlying the Bannister trope places at the centre of the four-minute mile myth a set of values that fuels a particular model of British character: determination, fighting back against the odds, *esprit de corps*, honour and national pride, fair play, decency, amateurism, grit in the face of adversity, golden moments in the greyness of the time. The Bannister, or four-minute mile, trope illustrates the way in which dominant cultures can make their own history, and contribute in turn to history's examination of their own historical worth.

## Notes

[1] Allen Guttmann, *Sports – The first five millennia* (Amherst, MA, 2004), p. 100.

[2] Richard Holt, *Sport and the British: A modern history* (Oxford, 1990), p. 279. More recently, Holt has referred to Bannister as a 'recent graduate' and a 'medical researcher' – Richard Holt, Race to glory, *Oxford Today,* 18(1), (2005), available online at http://www.oxfordtoday.ox.ac.uk/2005-06/v18n1/07.shtml, accessed 5 June 2006.

[3] John Bryant, *3:59.4: The quest to break the four-minute mile* (London, 2004), pp. 296–7.

[4] Ibid., pp. 297–8

[5] Ibid., p. 298.

[6] John Bale, 'Scientific and romantic: The rhetorics of the first four-minute mile', *International Journal of the History of Sport*, 21 (1) (2004), pp. 118–26.

[7] Neal Bascomb, *The perfect mile* (London, 2004), p. 315.

[8] Dole is quoted in Bob Phillips, *3:59.4: The quest for the four-minute mile* (Manchester, 2004), p. 13.

[9] Dole is quoted in S. Turnbull, 'The Bannister anniversary', *Independent on Sunday* (London), 2 May 2004, p. 7.

[10] See Raymond Williams, 'The analysis of culture', chapter 2 of *The long revolution* (London, 1961), p. 66.

[11] Compact edition of *The complete English dictionary* (complete text reproduced micrographically), Vol. 11, P–Z, supplement and bibliography (London, 1979), p. 3414.

[12] Ibid., p. 3415.

[13] *The Times* (London), 7 May 1954, p. 8.

[14] Ibid.

[15] Ibid.

[16] Chataway was speaking in the BBC Television programme *The first four minutes*, broadcast in May 2004.

[17] J. Rice, *1953: The crowning year of sport* (London, 2003), p. 7.

[18] Ibid.

[19] Ibid., p. 103.

[20] Ibid., p. 109.

[21] BBC Television, *The first four minutes*.

[22] Roger Bannister, *The first four minutes* (London, 1955), pp. 11–12.

[23] Bannister was speaking in *Six men and four minutes*, BBC Radio 4, 30 April 2004.

[24] BBC Radio 4, *PM*, 6 May 2004.

[25] Michael Sissons and Philip French, 'Introduction', in Michael Sissons and Philip French, eds., *Age of austerity – 1945–51* (Harmondsworth, 1964), p. 10.

[26] Susan Cooper, 'Snoek piquante – the trials and tribulations of the British housewife', in Sissons and French, *Age of austerity*, p. 37.

[27] Ibid., p. 57.

[28] James Walvin, *The only game: Football in our times* (London, 2001), p. 93; Peter Forster, 'J. Arthur Rank and the shrinking screen', in Sissons and French, *Age of austerity*, p. 288.

[29] Ivor Brown, ed., *The bedside 'Guardian' – a selection by Ivor Brown from the Manchester Guardian, 1951–1952* (London, 1952).

[30] Ibid., p. 184.

[31] Ibid., p. 183.

[32] Ibid., p. 185.

[33] Ibid.

[34] Ibid., p. 184.

[35] Morrison is quoted in Michael Frayn, 'Festival', in Sissons and French, *Age of austerity*, p. 334.

[36] Ibid., pp. 336–7.

[37] Ibid., p. 334.

[38] Sissons and French, *Age of austerity*, p. 12.

[39] Brian Glanville, 'Britain against the rest – the decline of British sporting prestige', in Sissons and French, *Age of austerity*, p. 172.

[40] B. Seebohm Rowntree and G.R. Lavers, *English life and leisure: A social study* (London, 1951).

[41] The Oxford newspapers consulted are the *Oxford Times*, 7 May 1954, and the *Oxford Mail*, 7 and 8 May 1954. I am indebted to Giles Moss for these references.

[42] *Burnley Express and News*, 8 May 1954, p. 13.

[43] *Cambridge Daily News* (night final), 7 May 1954, p. 16.

[44] Ibid.

[45] Ibid., p. 5.

[46] Ibid.

[47] Ibid.

[48] 'A backward glance at 1954', *Colne Times*, 7 January 1955, p. 6.

[49] Ibid.

[50] Juvenal, *The satires*, trans. Nial Rudd with introduction and notes by William Barr (Oxford, 1992), pp. 88–9.

[51] BBC Radio 4, *The tough of the track*, 30 July 2005.
[52] Peter and Paul Stanley, *The first four-minute mile and Tom Hulatt of Tibshelf* (Peterborough, 2004).
[53] Ibid., p. 79.
[54] *The Times*, 7 May 1954, p. 9.
[55] Jack Crump, 'Athletics – the last ditch in amateur sport', in Eamonn Andrews and Angus Mackay, eds., *Sportreport* (London, 1955), p. 167.
[56] Glanville, 'Britain against the rest', p. 170.
[57] 'Bannister and his mile – echoes of a great achievement', *The Times*, 8 May 1954, p. 4.
[58] Bale, Scientific and romantic', p. 124.
[59] Philip Carter, 'Myth, legend, and mystery in the *Oxford DNB*', *Oxford dictionary of national biography* (Oxford, 2004), available online at http://www.oxforddnb.com/themes/theme.jsp?articleid =92732, accessed 23 September 2005.
[60] Peter H. Hansen and Gordon T. Stewart, 'Debate – Tenzing's two wrist-watches: the conquest of Everest and late imperial culture in Britain 1921–1953', *Past and Present*, 157 (1997), p. 195.

# How Much of a Hero? The Fractured Image of Roger Bannister

John Bale

Roger Bannister's achievement of being the first man to run a mile in less than four minutes is widely regarded as one of the 'really important moments in sport'. [1] It has been claimed as an example of 'first great achievements which seem to open up new worlds of human possibility'. [2] It is this performance, that of the first runner to break the four-minute mile 'barrier', that has established Roger Bannister as a hero in the minds of many sports enthusiasts and many who know little about sport in, at least, the English-speaking world. It can be claimed that it was not solely this particular performance that contributed to Bannister's heroism since he had previously, in 1953, broken the British mile record. More importantly, in 1954 he also won the Empire title, defeating his successor as world mile record-holder, John Landy. In the same year he also won a gold medal at the European championships over 1,500 metres.

Additionally, Bannister's heroism may have derived from his 'amateur' image. Indeed, Lincoln Allison suggests that the 'gentleman athlete, as amateur and honest as the day is long' constitutes the 'Roger Bannister Syndrome'. [3] My main focus in this paper, however, is to explore the responses that were provoked by his world-record-breaking four-minute mile. In doing so I raise questions about the concept of the 'sports hero'.

The 'sports hero' has been the object of numerous explorations in the broad field of sports studies. [4] The polar extremes of attitudes to 'the sports hero' can be illustrated by two kinds of representations. On the one hand, for example, the sports historians Richard Holt and J.A. Mangan who, while recognizing the cultural relativism of the sports hero, feel comfortable arguing that 'a sport without a hero is like Hamlet without the prince' – in other words, a somewhat benign approach to heroism. [5] A positive view is also taken by studies of sports heroism that seek to set standards for the status of heroes. [6] Such standards, it has been suggested, have utilitarian value and can 'provide a reference for parents and others in selecting suitable role models for themselves and their children'. [7] On the other hand, the very notion of the sports hero has been read as a malign influence. Indeed, it has been suggested that the admiration of sports heroes contains fascistoid undertones, meaning, according to philosopher Torbjörn Tännsjö, that hero-worship and our admiration of victory and power carries with it a Nietzschean contempt for weakness. In other words, it is distasteful to admire those who are popularly known as heroes. [8] Likewise, Jeffrey Segrave notes that 'participation in sport may have negative impact on moral development', at worst infantilizing 'those who seek to derive sense and meaning from it'. [9] These different interpretations, of course, are simply examples of the *variety* of rhetorical modes that contribute to the overall composition of a discourse.

In this paper I do not seek to debate the merits and demerits of heroism *per se*. More important, I think, is the exploration of the textual construction of heroism and, of equal importance, how heroism is directly or indirectly contested. The contestation of heroic qualities confirms the fractured nature of 'heroism', a quality that is geographically and socially partial. Rarely is it asked *how* heroic one has to be in order to achieve the status of hero. Heroes often occupy specific social and/or geographical spaces: some adored Bannister and his four-minute mile; others disliked him and, at the same time, questioned the significance of the result. However, it is not my intention here to engage further in the formulation of a meaningful definition of the 'hero' which is, I believe, a sort of 'floating signifier' possessing a 'sliding of meaning' in its interpretation. [10]

The discourse – the collection of concepts, practices and statements involved in the production of knowledge about Roger Bannister – that makes up the collective response to the four-minute mile includes newspaper reports, journal articles, letters to editors and writing in books. This discourse has been constructed over a period of more than half a century. Additionally, it is an international discourse but it is highly fractured, not necessarily along British/non-British lines. It is the fractured nature of discourse of the four-minute mile that makes the notion of Bannister as hero problematic.

This paper is structured in four main sections. First, I provide a brief introduction to the running of the first four-minute mile. Secondly, I allude to what might be broadly termed positive responses to Bannister's achievement. A third section alludes to negative voices about the event and performance. A brief concluding section looks at the implications of the paper for the broader study of heroism in sports.

## Four minutes of fame

The first four-minute mile has been reported on many occasions. It seems unnecessary to deal here with the events leading up to the event, nor the precise details of the performance itself. [11] Of importance for this chapter is whether there was anything in the event itself that might justify or deny heroic status to Bannister.

The four-minute mile had been discussed from the beginning of the twentieth century. Numerous prognostications have made about ultimate athletic performances, including that for the mile. [12] By 1954 it was widely thought that the four-minute mile was overdue. The existing world record, made by the Swede Gunder Hägg, had been set as long ago as 1945. [13]. Because of the high expectations about the breaking of his record, the person who achieved it was likely to be held in high esteem. Put another way, because the four-minute mile was scarce, the prestige of the person who achieved it would be high. [14] It is questionable, however, whether the time period between the setting of Hägg's record and Bannister's world record was in any way unusual. For a substantial number of other athletic events, world records had stood still during the immediate post-war period.

The event that took place at Oxford's Iffley Road track on 6 May 1954 was a carefully planned 'experiment', a word used by Bannister to describe all his races. [15] And Bannister *was* a scientist. As such he transferred the language of the laboratory in which he worked to the running track. In a sense, he was setting out to test a model – the model of the four-minute mile. In order to do this in the most rational way he enrolled two friends, Chris Chataway and Chris Brasher, to be pacemakers. The term 'pacemaker' is derived from biochronology and has been defined as something for controlling or influencing rhythmic activity. [16] This is exactly what athletic pacemakers do. Bannister had already achieved results that strongly suggested that he would break the record. The other runners who made up the event were, on the one hand, the pacemakers and on the other, three runners who were there to legitimate the event as a *bona fide* competition. It was difficult to call this a 'race'. The planned performance involved Brasher leading for the first quarter-mile, Chataway assuming the pacemaker role until the final lap and then for Bannister to smoothly take the lead and break the record. This is what, indeed, happened. The experiment had been a success.

The so-called race has been described as an example of chivalry in which 'two first class athletes sacrificed themselves to permit Bannister to break a record'. [17] Additionally, it has been read as 'a triumph for the amateur spirit of British athletics, a team effort with a touch of undergraduate innocence'. [18] These sentiments, I think, require revision. True, it was a 'team effort' but also a division of labour. The monthly athletics magazine, *Athletics World*, which was published and edited by Norris and Ross McWhirter, close friends of Bannister, pointed out that to read the event as a 'sad sacrifice of the two Christophers' was a 'miserable misconception'. [19] Nobody but Bannister was going to win the race. Nor was the event innocent. Bannister, Chataway and Brasher had left their undergraduate years behind some years earlier and the Austrian émigré coach Franz Stampfl had been instrumental in organizing meticulously the strategy to be employed in breaking the record. [20] But it lasted only 46 days. In a race at Turku in Finland, it was bettered by Landy.

## Positive perceptions

The UK news media carried massive coverage of the four-minute mile. The event was front page – indeed, headline – news in most British newspapers. The reports of the race were invariably accompanied by a large photograph of Bannister breasting the tape. As Andrew Blake has noted, this 'crossover' of sport from back page to front page (except, in those days, *The Times*, of course), made the drama of the four-minute mile a truly public event, for a time displacing the routine stories of economics and politics. [21] The May issue of *Athletics World* was congratulatory. It included the most detailed report of the race that exists and a photograph of Bannister and Chataway, smiling at each other after the race. Dispensing with the comic convention of balloons coming out of the respective mouths, the caption read: 'Thanks Chris', 'Good show Roger'. [22]

And elsewhere, the accolades flowed freely. The Olympic 1,500 metres champion from Luxemburg, Joseph Barthel, congratulated Bannister with the words 'hard work pays'. [23] He did not read Bannister as a light trainer, an accusation that had been made about him in the British press two years earlier. Nor was he seen as a slacker in the USA. The *New York Times* remarked that 'his approach to running is coldly scientific'. [24] On the other hand, a well-known athletics coach, Brutus Hamilton, partly slipping into romantic 'Merrie England' mode, said: 'I'm glad Roger did it. The lad is a real amateur. He runs only because he loves to run. And he prepares himself well.' [25] Ken Doherty went further. Writing in *Scholastic Coach* he felt that Bannister's 'significance to sport lies in the fact that he is the *perfect amateur* and still beats the world'. [26] Veteran reporter Arthur Daley saw Bannister's record as 'trackdom's Holy Grail'. From an athletic, but also hyperbolic, standpoint, he added that 'this is as historic as the breaking of the sound barrier'. [27]

In later years Bannister was regularly presented in heroic terms. He features in *The book of British sporting heroes*; [28] he has his portrait in the National Portrait Gallery; and he is described as illustrative of 'the ethos of the English sporting gentleman'. [29] In the month leading up to 6 May 2004 Bannister was, for a while, resurrected as a national hero. Preceding the anniversary celebrations at Iffley Road, Oxford, three substantial hagiographic books were published that, broadly speaking, presented highly positive images of Sir Roger. For example, varying degrees of hagiography were found in the works of John Bryant and Neil Bascomb. The former states that there 'was a *national* delight' in Bannister's achievement'; Bascomb similarly quotes with approval the words of Lord Brabazon who observed that Bannister was 'an example to the world of our ideal sportsman'. [30]

The apogee of hero-worshipping Roger Bannister occurred in the 50th anniversary celebrations at Iffley Road on 6 May 2004. A day's festival of athletics took place. It was as much a social gathering as a sports event. It obtained considerable media coverage but hardly any world-class runners turned up to compete. The great and the good (and the not so good) of British athletics, including Chris Chataway and Jeffrey Archer, assembled to pay their congratulations to 50 years of the four-minute mile. The lavishly produced programme for the event, published by the University of Oxford public relations office, included a brief foreword by Her Majesty the Queen and a short essay by Chris Brasher. In it he averred that Roger Bannister's achievement must be placed alongside other big events of 1954. These included the creation of two new elements, Einsteinnium and Fermium by the US Atomic Commission, and the launching of the world's first atomic-powered vessel, the submarine *Nautilus*. [31] Hyperbole in sports writing was not unknown in the representation of Sir Roger.

## Negative noises

Between the euphoric and the condemnatory were neutral voices that saw the four-minute mile in a seemingly unbiased, almost disinterested way. Writing in the *Spectator*'s 'undergraduate' column, an Oxford student named Dudley Reeves referred to 'the sang-froid of the average Englishman' that followed the announcement of Bannister's world record run. Despite having been a spectator at the event, and accepting that he had witnessed 'the making of history', Reeves felt that:

> As we left the ground things came sweeping into perspective. There was a meal we must not miss, the writing of an essay we would dearly like to miss, sleep that awaited us at the end of the day and a score of other little things that constituted the daily round of common life. How after all if a mile were to be run faster one day? What sort of upstart goddess had men made for themselves in sport? Was it a sign of the time when a city noted for its academic achievements should secure fame through a purely athletic accomplishment? [32]

This sober view was likely to have been held by the majority of the population, especially those who were uninterested in sporting matters. At the same time, however, rather more strident, and clearly negative, views were expressed at the time and continued to (at least) the twenty-first-century celebrations at Iffley Road.

*Athletics Weekly*, the main voice serving British athletics fans, editorialized about the four-minute mile and provided a report on it. Here a more critical voice was heard, much less eulogistic than the national press and *Athletics World* which had been, more or less, part of the event. *Athletics Weekly* was the athletes' magazine and while the editor, P.W. Green, certainly congratulated the new world record holder he tempered his praise with a sense of reserve and even negation. Drawing on earlier criticism before and after Bannister's 'failure' in the 1952 Olympics (he finished fourth), Green sombrely stated that 'He has yet to win a race against world class opposition and running in cut-throat competition is very different to running in a race where one's competition is so helpful'. [33] *Athletics Weekly* carried a vigorous letters column. However, the number of letters printed about Bannister and the four-minute mile was relatively small and barely extended beyond the issue published the week after the event. This, of course, may have reflected the possibility that only a small number of letters about the four-minute mile were submitted. But even if this was the case, there were certainly more letters published a year earlier, on the question of whether athletics meetings should take place on Sundays and likewise concerning Bannister's earlier paltry response to the magazine's questionnaire, when his brief responses were seen as withholding information. [34]

One of the longest and strongest letters followed the line taken by the editor. It was far from unqualified praise. Yes, it was a great performance but things should be kept in perspective: 'Athletics should be a competitive sport, and that means competition against opponents, not merely against the clock.' [35] Bannister should undertake more racing and training and being a medical student was no excuse: 'You can't say you're the best miler until you've proved it in competition, Roger.' And Sydney Wooderson and Gordon Pirie had done far more for British athletics than Bannister had. Was this British self-loathing or an anti-Oxbridge tendency? It certainly saw Bannister as a less heroic light than that would be portrayed decades later. Harold Abrahams, hardly a radical when it came to sport, wrote in *The Listener* that there was always the danger that pacemaking spectacles such as that adopted on 6 May 1954 ran the danger of degenerating into 'stunts'. [36]

Nor was overseas reaction necessarily euphoric. In Australia, the reception was mixed. The leader comment in the *Sydney Morning Herald* reflected a stiff upper lip: 'Australians may be excused for wishing that the four-minute mile had fallen to Landy . . . but there is great consolation in the fact that the honour belongs, none the less, to the British Commonwealth.' However, there was a minor sting in the tail: 'But breaking 3.59 will be always seen, *quite unreasonably*, a lesser feat than breaking 4.00.' [37] Here the writer seemed to see the inevitability of Landy breaking Bannister's new world record, and it would be unreasonable to see it as any less heroic than Bannister's effort. However, some Australian press people and some athletes took a different line on Bannister's approach, which rumbled on for a couple of years. A couple of days after the record run, journalist Bruce Welch, writing in the Melbourne *Age*, noted that Landy had been handicapped from breaking the record 'by conditions, lack of competition and expert guidance'. [38] The Oxford result was said to have been achieved in 'artificial circumstances' [39] and was 'over-organized', [40] too planned, not a proper race. One particularly strident criticism came from the Australian correspondent of *Athletics World*, J.H. Galli. He observed that Landy (through Australian eyes, the epitome of the amateur sportsman) 'would never have been a party to such a schemed "race" as Bannister employed'. He (Landy) said repeatedly that he 'wanted to do it [the four-minute mile] "fair dinkum"'. [41] Bannister was seen to have unfairly benefited from pacemaking. Indeed, he acknowledged that he 'could not have done it without Chataway and Brasher'. [42]

That uncharitable Finnish genius, Paavo Nurmi, a former world-record-holder for the mile, was, as might be expected given his personality, curt and to the point: 'There's nothing unusual about a four-minute mile,' he said. 'It's only a question of intensified training.' [43] His compatriot, Denis Johansson, who was a contemporary of Bannister and a world-class middle-distance runner, was more scathing. 'What's Bannister done?' he asked, followed by his answer: 'Third in a European 800 metres championship' [44] (four years earlier).

Several 'experts' felt that the record would soon be broken, Santee and Landy being the obvious favourites. Now Bannister had done it, several US commentators thought it would become commonplace – and Bannister felt the same. Even the 1948 and 1952 Olympic 800 metres champion Mal Whitfield, who had no miling credentials and had failed to get anywhere near four minutes on a mile-long straight boardwalk in Atlantic City, New Jersey, stated that he could run 3m. 56.5s. The US coach Payton Jordan predicted that 'it's only a matter of time until they get the record down to 3m. 55s'. These coded messages verged on negation, implying that the four-minute mile was not that much of an achievement after all.

Occasional criticisms of Bannister continued well after his greatest performances had been achieved. In the mid-1960s, for example, the Australian coach Percy Cerutty stated that Bannister 'failed to achieved the pinnacle of greatness' by failing to break more world records or win an Olympic gold medal. [45] Bannister's limited number of supreme efforts per season was seen as 'a very immature approach' and he failed to 'perform at super-normal levels' in every race he ran. [46]

Fifty years after the first four-minute mile, negative voices were still audible. One strand of writing was even more critical than that of the 1950s and implicitly questioned the rationale of the 6 May 2004 junketing and commemoration, illustrating further the fractured nature of the

Bannister discourse. The first of these more critical views was a modest little publication that interestingly paid attention to the 'unknown' man who finished third, behind Bannister and Chris Chataway, in the world record race. His name was Tom Hulatt, a working-class runner from Tibshelf in Derbyshire who was – with Bannister, Chataway and Brasher – the other representative of the AAA team at the Oxford race in 1954. Although Hulatt obviously admired Bannister's record it is clear that he recognized the social distance between himself and every other competitor in the race. In particular, he disliked Bannister's attitude at the start of the race where he implied that Hulatt should keep out of the way of the 'team' that was attempting the record run. Hulatt was not one of them and he should know his place. Bannister was reported as saying to Hulatt 'Don't hang on to me and Chris [Chataway] – we are going all out. You run your own race.' Hulatt read the 'race' as a 'set up job', one in which he was there to simply make up the numbers. [47] Hulatt's is a poignant story. It seems clear to me that he was made to look a total outsider by all the other runners in the race, each of whom had an Oxbridge pedigree. Yet the ambivalence of heroism is reflected by the fact that despite the cold-shouldering by the Oxbridge set he looked up to Bannister. After the race he got his autograph that became one of his 'most treasured possessions'. [48]

The second strand in the 2004 discourse was made up of two newspaper articles that appeared in the week before 6 May. Each of then negated Bannister's record, claiming that the four-minute mile had been run before Bannister's well-known performance. [49] The first of these negations was published in *The Independent on Sunday* on 11 April. [50] It claimed that an athlete from Sheffield, Ken Wood, had run a mile in 3 minutes 59.2 seconds in training, 29 days before Bannister's world record result. Wood had been a world-class runner in the mid-1950s but little, if anything, was known about his alleged sub-four-minute mile until it was reported in *The Independent*. The report claimed that Wood's result was achieved in a solo time trial at the Sheffield University running track. Wood was adamant that the event had taken place. However, the 'evidence' of those who were associated with him at the time was unconvincing. Nevertheless, the report clearly countered the conventional wisdom of Roger Bannister as hero.

At about the same time a second newspaper article, written by Professor Peter Radford, appeared in *The Observer* and made an even more dramatic claim: that the first four-minute mile was run almost one hundred years before Bannister. [51] Radford looked back as far as 1770 when, at Shoreditch Church in London, a costermonger named James

Parrott was reported to have run a measured mile from Charterhouse Wall in Goswell Street in four minutes. Radford argued that this, and similar reports of four-minute miling by several other professional runners in the pre-modern era, had been censored by the amateur bureaucracies that came to control British athletics. Regardless of Radford's methodology and the reliability of his data, the article was explicitly or implicitly a negation of Bannister's record.

The final piece of counter-heroic writing about Bannister and the four-minute mile appeared in an article in *The Guardian* two days before the 6 May celebrations at Oxford. It was authored by the athletics writer and journalist Pat Butcher and is arguably the most critical of all the 2004 negativities that were aimed at Sir Roger. Butcher made the provocative claim that 'Bannister's run [was] one of the worst things that ever happened to athletics'. Far from being an admirable feat, it was 'cosy, conniving and dishonest. Its seminal contribution to sport has been to ruin middle-distance running worldwide.' [52] By this he meant that Bannister's use of pacemaking nurtured the belief that this was the only way to conduct middle-distance races. The implication was that Bannister had more or less invented pacemaking. The fact that this was not the case and that pacemaking had been a widespread practice at Oxbridge and among continental athletes [53] is irrelevant to this chapter since I am more interested in Bannister's representation than in 'historical fact'. Butcher also stated that it was not an 'honest competition' implying that it transgressed the norms of 'fair play'. [54]

There are, of course, several reasons to reject the kinds of observation reported in the previous three paragraphs. This, however, is not the point. What is of significance is that these critiques were all made in the week in which the 50th anniversary celebrations were taking place. They intentionally or unintentionally revealed an alternative reading of Bannister and the four-minute mile. They denied – or at least, contested – Bannister's heroic status.

## How heroic?

Heroes possess different constituencies. Bannister's reputation had always been fractured in the post-war milieu of British athletics. Well before the four-minute mile Bannister had attracted the admiration of those favouring the mythical Corinthian approach to athleticism. But he was also criticized in the early 1950s because of his reluctance to divulge his training methods; he was disliked for his predilection for running too few races; he was chastised for his penchant for pacemaking; and the

British press hammered him because of his relative 'failure' in the 1952 Olympics. [55] In other words, Bannister's career was littered with controversy, something that continued when his sporting career finished and is illustrated by his dubious comments about race and sport. [56] Such controversies contributed to counter-heroic sentiments by those who could find alternative heroes at a time when the United Kingdom possessed a number of alternative role models.

One of these heroes was Bannister's collaborator in the four-minute mile, Chris Chataway. He had, like Bannister, been an Oxford undergraduate. Four months after his pacemaking duties at Iffley Road, he contested a 5,000 metres race at the White City Stadium in London. In a meeting between London and Moscow his main opponent was Vladimir Kuts, the world record holder. In an exciting race, televised live by the BBC, Kuts led from the start, but was out-sprinted in the final metres by Chataway who won in a world-record time. Kuts regained the record ten days later. In the annual BBC 'Sports Personality of the Year' competition, it was Chataway who won, Bannister finishing in second place. There are several ways of reading what, at first sight, could be thought of a perverse result (e.g. the relative recentness of the race and its live television coverage). One thing it illustrates, however, is the ambivalence of Bannister's heroic status.

Gordon Pirie was another 1950s athlete who was also a contemporary of Bannister but attracted a different fan base. Pirie played the role of hero to middle-class, grammar school (or even secondary modern school) athletics fans. Whereas Bannister went out of his way to downplay the extent of his training and to deny that he possessed a coach, Pirie boasted about how much Zatopek-inspired training he did and was proud to announce that he 'gave himself' to German scientists who 'did his thinking for him'. [57] Pirie competed in three Olympic Games (winning a silver medal in one) and was a world-record holder at 3,000 and 5,000 metres. He achieved the world record in the 5,000 metres by defeating the holder, Vladimir Kuts, in a race held on a rainy evening in Bergen, Norway, in 1956. Pirie certainly was seen as a hero by a substantial segment of British athletics fandom, but he never quite received the publicity lauded on Bannister. He may have lacked the Oxbridge veneer; he may have been even more outspoken than Bannister; his best results were often achieved overseas; his social capital may have been formed from a different constituency. All heroism is relative and, like Pirie, perhaps all heroes are 'impossible' ones.

## Notes

[1] Andrew Blake, *The body language* (London, 1996), p. 196.

[2] Ibid.

[3] Lincoln Allison, *Amateurism in sport* (London, 2001), p. 37.

[4] See, for example, Robert Barney, 'The hailed, the haloed and the hallowed: Sport heroes and their qualities', in N. Muller and J. Ruhl, eds., *Sport history* (Reinhausen, 1987), pp. 88–103; Richard Holt, 'Champions, heroes and celebrities: Sporting greatness and the British public', in James Huntington-Whiteley, ed., *The book of British sporting heroes* (London, 1998); Alan Ingham, Jeremy Howell and Richard Swetman, 'Evaluating sport "hero/ines": Contents, forms, and social relations', *Quest*, 45 (1993), pp. 197–210; Jeffrey Segrave, 'Sport as a cultural hero-system: What price glory?', *Quest*, 45 (1993), pp. 182–96; Torbjörn Tännsjö, 'Is our admiration for sports heroes fascistoid?', *Journal of the Philosophy of Sport*, 25 (1998), pp. 23–34.

[5] Richard Holt and J.A. Mangan, 'Prologue: Heroes of a European past', in Richard Holt, J.A. Mangan and Pierre Lanfranchi, eds., *European heroes: Myth, identity and sport* (London, 1996), p. 4.

[6] Barney, 'The hailed, the haloed and the hallowed'.

[7] David Wenn, Merrill Melnick, Gordon Russell and Dale Pease, *Sport fans: The psychology and social impact of spectators* (New York, 2001), p. 70.

[8] Tännsjö, 'Is our admiration for sports heroes fascistoid?' For a critique of Tännsjö's thesis see Andrew Holowchak, '"Fascistoid" heroism revisited: A deontological twist in a recent debate', *Journal of the Philosophy of Sport*, 32 (1) (2005), pp. 105–115.

[9] Segrave, 'Sport as a cultural-hero system'.

[10] Stuart Hall, 'The work of representation', in Stuart Hall, ed., *Representation: Cultural representations and signifying practices* (London, 1997), p. 33.

[11] Detailed descriptions of the event can be found in *Athletics World*, May 1954; Roger Bannister, *The first four minutes* (London, 1955); and John Bale, *Roger Bannister and the four-minute mile* (London, 2004).

[12] See, for example, K.F. Dyer and T. Dwyer, *Running out of time: An examination of the improvement in running records* (Kensington, NSW, 1984).

[13] See Bale, *Roger Bannister*, p. 129.

[14] This approach to defining heroic status is adopted by William J. Goode, *The celebration of heroes: Prestige as a control system* (Berkeley, CA, 1978).

[15] Bannister, *The first four minutes*, p. 110.

[16] See D.N. Parkes and N.J. Thrift, *Times, spaces and place: A chronographic perspective* (Chichester, 1980).

[17] Richard Holt, *Sport and the British: A modern history* (Oxford, 1989).

[18] Richard Holt and Tony Mason, *Sport in Britain, 1945–2000* (Oxford, 2000).

[19] *Athletics World*, May 1954, p. 33. The magazine was inaugurated in March 1952 and ceased publication in February 1957.

[20] Although Stampfl's relationship to Bannister is ambiguous – and Bannister often denied that Stampfl was his 'coach' – Stampfl noted that 'Bannister was extremely reluctant to admit that he'd had any coaching from me. I thought at the time: "Well it doesn't matter. I'll prove I was the man"'. Brian Lenton, ed., *Through the tape* (Duffy, ACT, 1983), p. 108.

[21] Blake, *The body language*, p. 196.
[22] *Athletics World*, May 1954, p. 33.
[23] Ibid.
[24] *New York Times*, 7 May 1954, p. 5.
[25] Quoted in *Track and Field News*, May 1954, p. 5.
[26] Ken Doherty, 'Breaking through the four-minute barrier', *Scholastic Coach*, 24 (6) (1955), pp. 12–14, 42–43 (emphasis added). Whether Bannister was a 'perfect amateur' is debatable: See Bale, *Roger Bannister*.
[27] Quoted in *New York Times*, 7 May 1954, p. 5.
[28] Huntington-Whiteley, *The book of British sporting heroes*.
[29] Garry Whannell, *Fields in vision* (London, 1992), p. 191.
[30] John Bryant, *3:59.4: The quest to break the four-minute mile* (London, 2004), p. 289; Neal Bascomb, *The perfect mile* (London, 2004), p. 304.
[31] Chris Brasher, 'The Year 1954', in *50th Anniversary of Sir Roger Bannister's first four-minute mile* (Oxford, 2004), pp. 4–5.
[32] Dudley Reeves, 'The mile of the century', *The Spectator*, 14 May 1954, p. 591.
[33] *Athletics Weekly*, 22 May 1954, p. 3.
[34] For an overview of this debate see Bale, *Roger Bannister*, pp. 57–8.
[35] *Athletics Weekly*, 22 May 1954, p. 5 (letter from M.J. Chadwick).
[36] Harold Abrahams, *The Listener*, 13 May 1954, p. 833.
[37] Leading article, *Sydney Morning Herald*, 8 May 1954, emphasis added.
[38] Bruce Welch, 'Bannister has essential speed', *The Age*, 8 May 1954, p. 10.
[39] Ron Clarke and Alan Trengrove, *The unforgiving minute* (London, 1966), p. 41.
[40] Harry Gordon, *Young men in a hurry* (Melbourne, 1962), p. 205.
[41] J.H. Galli, *Athletics World*, June 1954.
[42] Quoted in *Track and Field News*, May 1954, p. 5.
[43] Quoted in *New York Times*, 7 May 1954, p. 4.
[44] Quoted in *Athletics Weekly*, 22 May 1954.
[45] Percy Cerutty, *Middle distance running* (London, 1964), p. 165.
[46] Ibid, pp. 15, 141.
[47] Peter and Paul Stanley, *The first four-minute mile and Tom Hulatt of Tibshelf* (Peterborough, 2004), p. 75.
[48] Ibid, p. 77.
[49] Many such claims have between made: see Bob Phillips, *3:59.4: The quest for the four-minute mile* (Manchester, 2004), pp. 103–4; Bale, *Roger Bannister*, p. 10.
[50] Simon Turnbull, 'The four-minute miler who beat Bannister by 29 days', *The Independent on Sunday*, 11 April 2004, p. 13 (Sportsweek).
[51] Peter Radford, 'The time a land forgot', *The Observer* (London), 2 May 2004.
[52] Pat Butcher, 'Completely off pace', *The Guardian*, 4 May 2004, p. 20. Butcher repeated these sentiments in his *The perfect distance – Ovett and Coe* (London, 2004).
[53] Bale, *Roger Bannister*.
[54] Butcher, 'Completely off pace'.
[55] Bannister, *The first four minutes*, pp. 160–1.
[56] On this subject see John Hoberman, *Darwin's athletes* (Boston, 1997), p. 144.
[57] Dick Booth, *The impossible hero* (London, 1999).

# Roger Bannister's American Image

Caroline Collins

In a National Public Radio broadcast aired in the USA on 28 April 2004, Frank Deford, now senior editor of *Sports Illustrated* magazine, described Roger Bannister as 'the last of his breed, the athlete on the side' and 'the last hero in sport': 'All that have followed, however great, have only been celebrities, stars, [and] superstars.' [1] If such remarks bespeak a growing disdain for the cult of the individual that pervades professional sports today, they also return us to the original context of the chase for the first four-minute mile. With the rules of amateur athletics becoming increasingly murky and more difficult to enforce in America and elsewhere, [2] Bannister's achievement of the four-minute mile was portrayed as the crown jewel of amateur athletics. American perception of Bannister's accomplishment at Iffley Road derives largely from this context, and it is in this context that his US image can be best examined and understood. By 'image,' I mean here the representation of athletes as interpreted and projected by the US print media, and also the effects of such representation on public perception in America.

The link between amateurism and heroism seemingly inherent in Bannister's May 1954 breaking of the coveted four-minute barrier remains central to his image everywhere, as Deford's commentary demonstrates. British media studies expert Garry Whannel has categorized Bannister as a 'good boy' (as opposed to a 'bad boy' or 'pretty boy'), and British sports historian Lincoln Allison has remarked upon the 'Roger Bannister syndrome', which carries connotations of sportsmanship, honesty, education and perspective, and also features athletics as both goal and way: an aim, but also an inspiration to other, more lofty pursuits. [3] In America, Roger Bannister's image as the heroic amateur developed partly in juxtaposition with the image of Wes Santee, the American contender in the race to the first four-minute mile. Initially heightened by contrast with Santee's apparent 'bad boy' persona, Bannister's 'good boy' image took on an additional lustre and the force of historical inevitability when Santee lost his amateur status and was written out of US distance-running history.

In America as elsewhere, the outpouring of nostalgia that accompanies the five- and ten-year anniversaries of the four-minute mile generally serves to reinforce Bannister's image as the miler destined for immortality. Recent American historical scholarship and literary efforts suggest, however, that Bannister's US image is changing: after more than four decades, American accounts of the race to the first four-minute mile have begun to include interviews with Wes Santee and others, probing Santee's image more deeply and dramatically restoring the four-minute mile to a close three-way race between Bannister, Santee and Australian runner John Landy. In the process, Bannister's American image is thus both subtly modified and actively revised.

For the Amateur Athletic Union (AAU) and some of the US media, even before the four-minute mile was achieved, Wes Santee had come to symbolize everything that was wrong with amateur athletics, while Bannister came to represent all that was right with it. Certainly Bannister's medical studies played a significant role in developing his 'good boy' image. As a medical student – at Oxford, no less – his participation in athletics resembled a pastime much more closely than a profession. In addition, the ability to double at the track as attending physician for a photographer injured by a javelin in July 1953 enhanced Bannister's image as the ultimate amateur for whom sport was, quite properly, only one small part of life. [4] Yet, as John Bale has pointed out, Bannister's autobiographical account of the four-minute mile betrays a tension between a romantic notion of amateur athletics, in which the 'joy in struggle' proved its own reward, and a seemingly professional, aggressively scientific approach, in which each training run and race became 'an experiment'. [5] In reality, the distinction between amateur and professional was far more complex than the American media's portraits suggested.

Santee had already emerged as a 'bad boy' hero in the US months before Bannister achieved the four-minute mile. According to the 1953 *Track and Field News* and recent historical accounts, Santee and US half-miler Mal Whitfield had asked a German track official about the possibility of exchanging several unopened small prizes for a camera during the summer of 1953, while competing abroad on an AAU tour. [6] When the official reneged, a disagreement ensued. After the official complained in writing, the AAU began an investigation into the amateur status of both runners, conducting its study with such secrecy that many in the media automatically assumed illegal payoffs were involved: an *Atlanta Constitution* story, compiled from wire reports, notes that Whitfield had been 'charged with demanding excessive expenses' but was eventually 'cleared of suspicion'. [7]

From the outset, some US track fans questioned the validity of the investigation. Coaches and fans who had been close to the athletes during the summer tour offered brief character references, which appeared in the September and October 1953 issues of *Track and Field News*. [8] But the extended inquiry into Santee's amateur status eventually took a toll on his image. Santee's name, along with Whitfield's, was withdrawn from consideration for the Sullivan Award, an AAU honour presented annually to the athlete 'who, by his or her performance, example, and influence as an amateur, has done the most during the year to advance the cause of sportsmanship'. [9] By 1953, the Sullivan award had come to reflect the murkiness of amateur athletics in America, with such issues as 'sportsmanship' and 'character' taking on increasing significance. The eventual 1953 winner, Sammy Lee, was described on the AAU ballot as 'a courageous competitor, a true sportsman and a man of integrity and high ideals'. [10] Lee, who had been runner-up for the 1952 award, was a two-time Olympic platform diving champion. To the AAU, he exemplified the virtues of amateur athletics and no one questioned his character or sportsmanship. An ear, nose and throat specialist serving in the armed forces at a hospital in Korea, Lee was certainly a popular choice. However, because he had not competed at all that year, he had hardly met the award's first criteria, that of 'performance'. Lee was in fact the first athlete to receive the Sullivan award without having taken part in a national championship during the year of his selection, and the AAU's inconsistency in this matter raised some objections.

Writing after the winner had been announced in December, Cordner Nelson of *Track and Field News* objected that the AAU had vastly overplayed the always ill-defined qualitics of sportsmanship and character. He noted that previous recipients had been lauded strictly 'for their athletic ability and for only as much sportsmanship as thousands of athletes show every year'. Moreover, he added, a good number of winners had been 'experts' at successfully lobbying for increased expenses and more valuable prizes. [11] The four 'write-in' votes Santee received for the Sullivan award indicate that he retained a certain amount of popularity with the press in spite of the controversy. Yet, as the investigation into his amateur status dragged on, it occupied a great deal of media attention. Moreover, in his remarks to the press, AAU secretary-treasurer Dan Ferris portrayed Santee as increasingly troubled and difficult, thus justifying the exclusion of the young miler from a tribute 'based on sportsmanship and character as well as ability'. [12] Questions about sportsmanship and character would continue to play a crucial part in American perceptions and judgments of 1950s athletes, and in particular their perceptions of Wes Santee.

Santee's media image took yet another hit in September 1953 when an ill-timed article entitled 'Sure, I'll run the four-minute mile' appeared in the *Saturday Evening Post*. The story inadvertently coupled the young miler's desire to collect 'expenses' with his goal of eventually purchasing a farm – a matter cleared up only after the author wrote to the AAU himself, claiming responsibility for the unfortunate inference and emphasizing that Santee had said nothing to indicate such a connection. [13] The piece also portrayed Santee as virtually sure that he would reach four minutes first: 'I don't know when it will be . . . but I'll run it, you can be sure of that. I'm as certain I can run the four-minute mile as you are that you can drive your car home.' [14] Although television would later render the often witty repartee between interviewer and athlete, conveying a dimension of the athlete's personality seldom captured in newspaper and magazine accounts, it did not become the dominant medium in the US until the 1960s, and its coverage of athletics in the early 1950s was minimal. [15] Santee's extroverted, wisecracking personality doubtless came across well in the television exposure he received. But in the midst of the AAU's serious, secretive inquiry and in the great conformity and conservatism of 1950s America, his outspoken confidence translated poorly into the US print media.

Bannister, by contrast, was depicted by the US print media as almost awkwardly shy, possessing a reserve that had become part of his American image as early as 1951, prior to his competition in the Benjamin Franklin mile. Despite having lowered his mile time to 4:09, he '*modestly* declined comment as to his chances' against top American milers Don Gehrmann and Fred Wilt. [16] Because of his apparent effortlessness during the race and his refusal to gloat afterwards, Bannister's post-race remarks also came across as self-effacing: '"I think it could easily have been a 4:05 if there had been a faster pace," Bannister said, *not boastingly*.' [17]

Within a few years, Bannister, Santee and Landy all seemed poised on the threshold of the four-minute mile: the question was who would get there first. In February 1954, Santee's chances of being the first were suddenly diminished when the AAU announced that it would ban four track and field athletes, including Santee, from international competition for one year, as punishment for 'breaking training and curfew rules' while competing abroad the previous summer. [18] Neal Bascomb, the American who authored *The perfect mile*, a 2004 revisionist history of the chase to the first four-minute mile, clarifies the severity of the ruling and its impact on Santee: 'Not only could he not go there [abroad], they [international runners] couldn't come here [to America] and compete with him.' [19] Perhaps more importantly, Santee earned the enmity of the AAU and some in the US press with his public denial of the charges and his angry denunciations: 'I no more broke training than I flew the Atlantic without an airplane. . . . Why don't they show some courage and nail me, if they have to . . . for what they're really sore about – the fact that I told off some of their foreign officials.' [20] In a 1999 article about Santee's struggle to break four minutes and his battles with the AAU, sports historian Joseph Turrini notes that American athletes' problems with the AAU date back to 1930. [21] He also traces Santee's vocal response to the one-year ban back to earlier events, including the AAU's refusal to allow him to compete in both the 1,500 and 5,000 metres at the trials for the 1952 Helsinki Olympics and its insistence that he extend his 1953 summer tour by an additional six weeks – to placate international officials who allowed 'second-tier' American athletes to take part in their meets only if 'top draw' athletes such as Santee and Whitfield also competed. [22] In the conservative social climate of the time, some American press members apparently interpreted Santee's reaction as an unseemly private war against authority. Not surprisingly, his image suffered accordingly. As historian William H. Young explains in his book on 1950s America, 'Extremism and dissent had little voice in popular culture, and those challenging the status quo usually saw themselves depicted in a negative way.' [23]

Set against this anti-amateur, 'bad boy' image of Santee in the American press, Bannister's achievement of the four-minute mile took on increased significance. Indeed, the initial laudatory US responses to Bannister's triumph at Iffley Road, which appeared in newspapers and magazines across the country, also serve to idealize and defend amateur athletics, and are thus most fully appreciated when restored to this original context. University of California coach Brutus Hamilton's declaration that the British runner 'runs only because he loves to run' vastly oversimplified Bannister's approach in order to advance the goals of amateur athletics; [24] journalist Maxwell Stiles's pronouncement that 'in many ways, he [Bannister] was the most deserving' speaks to the image of the British runner as a busy medical professional, obliged to squeeze in his brief training whenever he could find time for it, between many other duties. [25] Perhaps *Newsweek* magazine most clearly reflects the emphasis on amateur athletics, with its depiction of Bannister as the quintessential Renaissance man: remarkably, he becomes the '25-year-old medical student, pianist, painter, amateur actor, and dancer' whose monumental achievement 'turned the gloom to gloating', single-handedly averting the grim post-war malaise that had enveloped England. [26]

From May 1954 on, then, the US print media depicted Bannister as the one who best embodied the sacrosanct values of amateur athletics and the spirit of the age. Members of the American press who had already connected Wes Santee with a spirit of anti-amateurism did not miss the opportunity to take their aim. *Atlanta Constitution* sportswriter Furman Bisher begins his description of Bannister's four-minute feat with a seemingly comic tone: 'While Wes Santee fiddled, a clock-watching Englishman wearing an outboard motor burned up a track . . . Thursday.' [27] Yet the portrayal of the American miler as insouciant emperor soon becomes less playful: indeed, in its implication that Santee might be guilty of laziness – a charge frequently levelled against young people at the time – the article intimates the intra-generational conflict simmering under the surface of 1950s America. [28] Moreover, the evocation of Nero takes on a more sinister tone when traced back to Santee's earlier statement about running – 'I just don't like to fiddle around' – which had been printed in the *Saturday Evening Post* story the previous fall. [29] Bisher interprets John Landy's reaction that he 'just wasn't the man for the job' of lowering Bannister's new mark as an attractive humility – a welcome contrast to Santee. Chronicling Santee's rise in the mile and his levelling-off, Bisher evokes anonymous critics: 'He ran and ran, and some experts said he was running too much, burning himself out. Some of them, a little miffed at the untoward attitude of the Santee boy, spoke up and said that if he didn't make it, it would be nobody's fault but his own.' [30]

Because Bannister himself has since used the space race as a metaphor for the public's fervour about the four-minute mile, it is tempting to read in Bisher's tone the same cold war rhetoric that marked America's disappointment after the Soviet launch of Sputnik. Yet the four-minute mile had never before figured prominently in the *Atlanta Constitution*, still a fairly small daily newspaper in 1954. Ongoing assaults on the mile record had been noted, but scarcely followed up in detail: Bannister's achievement is news only because he broke four minutes. And although the article's title, 'Dark star with two legs,' colourfully recalls the previous year's Kentucky Derby, when Dark Star overpowered the favourite, Native Dancer, beating odds of 25 to 1, Bisher's analogy does not really hold. For close followers of track and field in America, Bannister was hardly a dark horse or long shot. In fact, he was probably the first to excite speculation about the four-minute mile in the US, when his decisive victory in the 1951 Penn Relays mile prompted an anonymous track official to call him 'the first man I've seen I think capable of a four-minute mile'. [31] By February 1954, Cordner Nelson of *Track and Field News* had accurately whittled the four-minute mile down to a three-way contest between Bannister, Santee and Landy, with Sune Karlsson and Stanislav Jungwirth as dark horses; he viewed Bannister as a longer shot than the others strictly because his ability to work himself up for only a few races a year diminished his chances of running four minutes flat. [32] Readers of *Track and Field News* also had probably deduced, from an announcement in the November 1953 issue, that Bannister would not be racing much that winter due to his hospital duties. [33] Having been aware of his potential since his first American competition in 1949, however, they would not have ruled him out of any mile race, especially the one to the first four-minute mile. For Bisher, though, Bannister's four-minute mile is most significant as a symbol of amateur athletics – a fitting antithesis for the growing movement towards individualism and professional sports personified by Santee's rebellious outspokenness. The writer's point is certainly clear: Bannister gets the four-minute mile, and Santee gets his comeuppance.

Not long after Bannister's famous 3:59.4, Santee improved Gunder Hägg's 1,500 metres world record on his way to a 4:00.6 mile, but his feat meant little in an era obsessed with breaking four minutes and in a country with no frame of reference for the metric system. In the *New York Times*, his new mark merited neither front-page status nor a picture on the sports page, though *Track and Field News* noted that it made headlines throughout Europe. [34] Santee's accomplishment would soon be further obscured when John Landy broke Santee's new record on his way to shattering Bannister's sub-four mile several weeks later.

Ironically, even Landy faced an uphill battle against Bannister's media image in America. Bettering Bannister's mile time by 1.4 seconds in early July made Landy front-page news in the *New York Times* and landed his picture on the sports page, but the coverage was not entirely laudatory. The sports editorial about Landy's new mile record is entitled 'It's getting to look easy', and his photo is relegated to the bottom of the page, while the British runner's graces the top, with the words 'Roger Bannister: He did it first' beneath. [35] As early as 1949, just before Bannister's first US competition, sportswriter Arthur Daley had ranked him with such 'so-called sleepers from the Empire' as Oxbridge runners Harold Abrahams, Jack Lovelock and others who had 'first served notice' and 'planted their feet on the highroad to immortality' in the same series of meets against Harvard-Yale and Princeton-Cornell. [36] Bannister joined this lineage not by virtue of his best mile time, but because his lean build, strong finish, Oxford medical studies and refusal to run faster than necessary recalled the great Jack Lovelock, who had competed against Princeton. Because Daley had predicted that four-minute miles would become commonplace after Bannister, the Australian's feat is thus viewed as an expected, unsatisfying denouement. Bannister's subsequent defeat of Landy in the Empire Games mile, his willingness to serve as attending physician to British marathon runner Jim Peters, his early retirement from track, his autobiography and his knighthood further refined and sealed his 'good boy' media image, in the US and elsewhere. It should perhaps be added here that Arthur Daley eventually penned two glowing reviews of Bannister's autobiography, one for the *New York Times* book review section, and one that appeared as a sports editorial (and incidentally recommended that Wes Santee might find the Briton's volume potentially helpful for his racing strategy). [37] Bannister's subsequent achievements and honours, whether related to medicine or sports, were noted dutifully in *Track and Field News* as well as prominent mainstream publications.

Wes Santee, on the other hand, was soon embroiled in his third and final conflict with the AAU. He continued to compete while serving in the armed forces after college, but in 1955, the governing body began another investigation of his amateur status, this time for accepting 'expenses' that exceeded its prescribed limits. Unwilling to withdraw quietly, the miler took the AAU to court. Reactions to Santee's battle to retain his amateur standing were complex and varied. Cordner Nelson of *Track and Field*

*News* dismissed the runner's objections about the misconduct of the governing body and other athletes as 'immature begging of the question'. [38] In *Athletics World* magazine, Bannister's pals Norris and Ross McWhirter pointed to secretary-treasurer Dan Ferris's devoted service to amateur athletics over the course of three decades, denouncing the 'arrogance' that had led Santee to 'flout the rules' of the AAU. [39] The ensuing showdown was long, ugly and well publicized; former and then current US athletes argued that accepting expenses beyond the AAU's stringent limits was a common and necessary practice, and the media decried the fall of amateurism. Not surprisingly, Santee's image in the print media declined swiftly. In the *New York Times*, the American miler's picture flanked Arthur Daley's editorial entitled 'What Price Amateurism?' Just as Bannister's four-minute mile at Iffley Road had provided a clear symbol of the virtues of amateur athletics, in America Wes Santee's struggle to retain his amateur status enabled the AAU and the US press to put a face on poor sportsmanship and the evils of anti-amateurism. In the absence of clear parameters to define amateurism, Santee's case offered a convenient way to emphasize strongly what amateur athletes should not do. Both Arthur Daley and Cordner Nelson applauded the AAU's determination to stick to its high principles. Citing Santee's tremendous popularity with fans, they interpreted the governing body's decision to sideline 'its hottest gate attraction' and thus 'forfeit much-needed dollars' as a show of 'great moral courage in the face of formidable popular opinion'. [40] When Santee won a temporary injunction from the New York State Supreme Court, which allowed him to continue competing until the final outcome of the trial was near, the AAU declared that anyone who competed with him faced great peril and revoked the amateur status of the entire College of William and Mary team when two of its athletes raced against him. A number of meet directors organized separate heats for those reluctant to anger the AAU. Eventually, few athletes except Santee's fellow servicemen were willing to risk such 'contamination rules'. [41] After Santee refused to testify on his own behalf or to allow fellow athletes to do so – on the grounds that either move would severely compromise the quality of the 1956 US Olympic team – the AAU's lawyer accused him of 'conduct unbecoming to any athlete, any citizen, any officer, and any soldier': clearly the opposite of the ideal amateur, hero or sportsman. [42]

Santee was permanently banned from amateur competition on 16 May 1956, roughly two years after Bannister's famous feat at Iffley Road. Like Santee's short-lived 1,500-metre record, the news made headlines around the world. [43] Several months later, his detailed account of illegal payoffs – including dates, locations, amounts received and names of AAU officials – appeared in *Life* magazine. This willingness to expose the corruption within the AAU further damaged Santee's image with the American media. In his closing comments he averred that '[i]f I had it to do over, I would follow the same pattern, which others in my position have followed for 25 years'. [44]

Perhaps in the minds of some, Santee's adamant stance justified his banishment. Yet he retained his popularity with fans, who came down overwhelmingly on his side. A telephone poll in California found that only one in 4,639 Americans agreed with the AAU's decision – odds that suggest that they were already aware of the 'underground-labour-relations system' that his battle for his amateur status exposed. [45] After his dramatic fall from grace, the American miler was eventually written out of American sports history. A prominent newsman and track and field fan anonymously described Santee as the AAU's 'sacrificial goat' in a subsequent issue of *Track and Field News*, and some called for the formation of a new governing body, but their objections were based largely on the shoddy officiating and organizing of the AAU annual meet rather than its treatment of Santee. [46] It is doubtful that he reappeared in any of the nostalgic 'Remember?' photos that offer flashbacks to previous American triumphs in *Track and Field News*. Santee has been essentially consigned to oblivion – or at least shunned. In an article about US miling prospects, carefully timed to coincide with the golden jubilee of Bannister's four-minute mile, current CEO of US Track and Field and one-time 3:52.02 miler Craig Masback notes that Americans 'have never been any good in the 1,500'. [47] Although he names a few 'occasional outstanding performers', Santee is not among them; for anyone aware of his briefly held 1,500 metres record, the absence seems conspicuous. Bannister's achievement of the four-minute mile, by contrast, has gathered the force of historical inevitability. Generations of Americans, even non-sports fans, readily recall the media attention and public interest generated by the first four-minute mile. A subsequent generation, members of the 'first wave' of the baby boom that stretched from 1946 to 1964 – who were too young to be aware of the event or had not yet been born when Bannister achieved his four minutes of fame – read about his triumph in Childcraft readers during their grammar-school years. American coaches also passed the story of Bannister's 3:59.4 mile to generations of young runners. [48] Wes Santee was not a part of that story.

Yet Americans have recently begun to learn about Santee, from accounts of the four-minute mile in *Sports Illustrated* and on the *History*

*Channel*. Two years ago, it was difficult to find Santee anywhere on the Internet. Now, it seems, he is everywhere: the 45th and 50th anniversaries of the four-minute mile have brought him out of obscurity in his home country. Bannister's image has thus been revised, both subtly and not so subtly, in recent American accounts of the race to the first four-minute mile. Joseph Turrini's 1999 account of Santee's struggle to break four minutes presents him as a successor of the US athletes who had fought the AAU in the 1930s and as a courageous predecessor of the US track and field athletes who successfully took up the battle against corruption in the AAU in the 1970s and early 1980s. [49] Thus Santee may now be read as one whose intrepid candour would likely have made him a cultural hero in the turbulence of 1960s and 1970s America, but was greatly at odds with the conservatism and conformity that characterized his country in the 1950s.

Neal Bascomb's 2004 book *The perfect mile* enlarges on Turrini's work, depicting the four-minute mile as a close and exciting three-way race between Bannister, Landy and Santee. Offering more detailed portraits than ever before of the international rivals who helped push the British runner to four minutes, Bascomb's narrative thus enacts a more active and dramatic revision of Bannister's image. As with the May 1954 portrayals of the British runner, Santee is now depicted as struggling to balance his other obligations with the necessary time for training. Moreover, his close friendship with African-American half-miler Mal Whitfield emerges as a heroic defiance of a social taboo: unlike many American athletes who continued to abide by the racial segregation imposed in 1950s America even when they were not at home, Santee roomed with Whitfield while they competed abroad. [50] Other social factors figure in as well. As the child of an abusive and exploitative father, having grown up with a far less privileged life than Bannister or Landy, Santee was also the first four-minute mile contender to take on the responsibilities of marriage. [51]

We are perhaps better able to appreciate Bannister's achievement when the race to the first four-minute mile is placed in its original context as a three-man race. Certainly *The perfect mile* demonstrates that Santee and Landy laboured under stricter rules about pacing, enforced by a stricter governing body. Bascomb thus exposes the initial, somewhat misleading 'lone wolf' image of Bannister remarked upon in initial US accounts of his Iffley Road triumph – in the areas of management and public relations as well as training, pacing and coaching. [52] Among other things, the narrative depicts how, with the help of close friends Norris and Ross McWhirter, Bannister was able to 'hand-pick' his competitors for arranged 'secret' or low-key meets – which was not possible for Santee or Landy. [53] Bascomb also illuminates the efforts of the McWhirters to eliminate obstacles that had tripped up other milers. For example, after Landy had been unable to hear his quarter-mile splits, the pair arranged to have amplifiers hooked up to a microphone to make sure Bannister could hear his. [54] Set against the efforts of the rivals who also strived to reach the four-minute mile, one can certainly view Bannister as having the best of both worlds, at least in terms of management and public relations: had he failed in his May 1954 bid at Iffley Road, the publicity would have been minimal. Yet, with the McWhirters present, he also had in place a fail-proof system for getting the word out to the rest of the world, upon a successful attempt. By contrast, Santee and Landy, whose attempts on the four-minute mile were highly publicized before each competition, had nowhere to hide when they fell short.

Bannister's 1995 announcement of his theory that black athletes in general and sprinters in particular 'seem to have certain natural anatomical advantages' scarcely dented his image in America, probably because he had virtually retired from practising medicine at the time. It is perhaps worth noting that some in the US press read his bluntness as a blow against a prevailing attitude of political correctness. [55] In recent years, Bannister's 'good boy' image has received impetus in America and elsewhere from his significant role in developing the drug tests that resulted in Canadian Ben Johnson being stripped of his Olympic gold medal for the 100-metre dash and from his public support of increased drug testing for athletes. [56] Interestingly, in his brief preface to John Bryant's 2004 volume, *3:59.4: The Quest to Break the Four-Minute Mile*, the British runner evokes the wrongdoing of his American nemesis: '[W]e can almost sympathise with Santee's problem of gazing at a collection of 57 watches, the usual prize for helping to fill a stadium with some 20,000 spectators.' [57] Fifty years later, his greatness clearly established, Bannister defines himself by contrast with Santee, just as the US press did. Whether he is motivated by the continuing difficulties of defining amateurism without falling back on ethics or a concern for his own changing image, Bannister's commentary summons the rigid, clear-cut moral distinctions of 1950s America. Perhaps it also suggests an awareness, on his part, that a hero requires a villain.

If, as John Bale has suggested, we can see Bannister as a 'pre-modern' runner, slightly out of place or ahead of his time because of an emphasis on training, science, and records, [58] perhaps we may now view Santee as equally out of place, a pre-modern or even pre-professional runner whose drive and aggressive, outspoken individuality prefigured the move away from amateur athletics and towards professional sports. In placing

Bannister mid-stride, beside Santee and Landy, the most recent American accounts serve to modify Bannister's image in the US by demonstrating that although the four-minute mile was inevitable, it was not inevitable that Bannister would be the first to attain it. With their contrasts, such narratives remind us that Bannister's accomplishment did not take place in a vacuum. They also provide an apt counterbalance to the growing nostalgia and force of historical inevitability that now mark each anniversary of the first four-minute mile.

## Notes

[1] Frank Deford, 'Roger Bannister's achievement of the four-minute mile without the help of a coach or steroids', *Morning Edition* (Bob Edwards, host), National Public Radio, Washington DC, 28 April 2004, p. 1, ProQuest online database, Gordon College Lib., accessed 20 Sept. 2004. For other commentary by Frank Deford on Roger Bannister, see 'Bannister and Hillary', *Sports Illustrated*, 27 Dec. 1999, p. 64.

[2] Joseph Turrini, 'Wes Santee, the four-minute mile, and the Amateur Athletic Union of the United States', *Sports History Review*, 1999, p. 67.

[3] Garry Whannel, *Media sports stars* (London, 2002), pp. xiii, 99–100; John Bale, *Roger Bannister and the four-minute mile* (London, 2004), pp. 1–2; Lincoln Allison, *Amateurism in Sport*, (Portland, OR, 2001), p. 37.

[4] 'Bannister scores in 4:05.2 mile run', *New York Times*, 12 July 1953, p. 3.

[5] Roger Bannister, *The four minute mile* (Guildford, 1981), pp. 59, 113; John Bale, 'Scientific and romantic: The rhetorics of the four-minute mile', *International Journal of the History of Sport*, 21 (2) (2004), pp. 118, 123.

[6] Jack Clowser, 'Record planned for Wes', *Track and Field News*, Jan. 1954, p. 5; Turrini, 'Wes Santee', pp. 63–4; Neal Bascomb, *The perfect mile* (Boston, 2004), pp. 135–7.

[7] 'Coast official clears Whitfield of AAU charges', *Atlanta Constitution*, 16 Dec. 1953, p. 26.

[8] Bert Nelson, 'So they tell me', *Track and Field News*, Sept. 1953, p. 12; Bert Nelson, 'So they tell me', *Track and Field News*, Oct. 1953, p. 7; Cordner Nelson, 'Track Talk', *Track and Field News*, Dec. 1953, p. 6; Jack Clowser, 'Record planned for Wes', p. 5.

[9] 'The Sullivan Award: History', *HickokSports.com*, 17 Nov. 2004, available online at www.hickoksports.com/history/sulaward.shtml, accessed 17 Nov. 2004.

[10] 'Sammy Lee wins Sullivan award', *Atlanta Constitution*, 31 Dec. 1953, p. 6.

[11] Cordner Nelson, 'Track Talk', *Track and Field News*, Dec. 1953, p. 6.

[12] Bascomb, *The perfect mile*, pp. 151, 293 n.151.

[13] Turrini, 'Wes Santee', p. 64.

[14] Bob Hurt, 'Sure, I'll run the four-minute mile', *Saturday Evening Post*, Sept. 1953, p. 136.

[15] Edward J. Rielly, *The 1960s* ('American popular culture through history' series) (Westport, CT, 2003), p. 193.

[16] William J. Briordy, 'Bannister, Britain's star miler, here to compete in Penn Relays', *New York Times*, 23 April 1951, p. 30.
[17] 'Bannister hailed for mile triumph', *New York Times*, 30 April 1951, p. 26 (italics added).
[18] Joseph Sheehan, 'AAU disciplines four track aces', *New York Times*, 22 Feb. 1954, p. 23.
[19] Neal Bascomb, telephone interview, 20 Aug. 2004.
[20] Bascomb, *The perfect mile*, pp. 158, 293 n.158.
[21] Turrini, 'Wes Santee', pp. 61, 80 n.43.
[22] Ibid., pp. 59–61, 63.
[23] William H. Young (with Nancy K. Young), *The 1950s* ('American popular culture through history' series) (Westport, CT 2004), p. 5.
[24] 'Bannister: His day of days', *Track and Field News*, May 1954, p. 5.
[25] Ibid., p. 5.
[26] 'The miracle mile', *Newsweek*, 17 May 1954, p. 57.
[27] Furman Bisher, 'Dark star with two legs', *Atlanta Constitution*, 8 May 1954, p. 5.
[28] Young, *The 1950s*, p. 23.
[29] Hurt, 'Sure, I'll run the four-minute mile', p. 137.
[30] Ibid., p. 5.
[31] 'Track experts see Bannister as no. 1 miler of all time', *New York Herald-Tribune*, 30 April 1951, p. 22.
[32] Cordner Nelson, 'Track Talk', *Track and Field News*, Feb. 1954, p. 3.
[33] 'On your marks', *Track and Field News*, Nov. 1953, p. 11.
[34] Cordner Nelsson, 'Santee runs 4:00.6', *Track and Field News*, June 1954, p. 3.
[35] Arthur Daley, 'It's getting to look easy', *New York Times*, 22 June 1954, p. 31.
[36] Ibid., 'On the international front', *New York Times*, 10 June 1949, p. 37.
[37] Ibid., 'What made Roger run', *New York Times* (book review section), 13 Nov. 1955, p. 20; Ibid.., 'Back on the merry-go-round', *New York Times,* 2 Feb. 1956, p. 33.
[38] Cordner Nelson, 'Track Talk', *Track and Field News*, Feb. 1956, p. 9.
[39] Bob Phillips, *3:59.4: The quest for the four-minute mile* (Manchester, 2004), p. 174.
[40] Arthur Daley, 'What price amateurism?' *New York Times*, 2 Nov. 1955, p. 45; Cordner Nelson, 'Track Talk', *Track and Field News*, Feb. 1956, p. 9.
[41] Turrini, 'Wes Santee', p. 86–7 n.168.
[42] Ibid., pp. 75, 86 n.176.
[43] 'Story without a hero', *Newsweek,* 5 March 1956, pp. 86–7.
[44] 'Wes Santee, "Names, dates and payoffs: Santee blows the whistle"', *Life Magazine*, Nov. 1956, p. 110.
[45] 'Story without a hero', p. 86; Turrini, 'Wes Santee', p. 57.
[46] Bert Nelson, 'So they tell me', *Track and Field News*, Feb. 1956, p. 8.
[47] 'Is there hope for US milers', *USA Today*, 6 May 2004, p. 1.
[48] Jim Denison, *Bannister and beyond: The mystique of the four-minute mile* (Halcottsville, NY, 2003), pp. 91, 146, 187.
[49] Turrini, 'Wes Santee', pp. 76–7, 86 n.189.
[50] Bascomb, *The perfect mile*, p. 25.
[51] Ibid., pp. 20–4, 149, 167–8.

[52] Ibid., pp. 120–1, 131–4, 160–2, 178–80, 289 n.121; 'Britain's Bannister runs world record 3:59.4 time', *Chicago Tribune*, 7 May 1954, p. 2.

[53] Bascomb, *The perfect mile*, pp. 131–4, 160–2, 178–80.

[54] Ibid., p. 186.

[55] Dave Kindred, 'You can't be color blind', *Sporting News*, 219 (1995), pp. 1–2; Jack McCallum and Kostya Kennedy, 'Another race for Sir Roger', *Sports Illustrated*, 25 Sept. 1995, p. 1.

[56] Jack Cavanagh, 'Bannister favors more drug testing', *New York Times*, 7 May 2000, p. 1.

[57] Roger Bannister, 'Preface', in John Bryant, *3.59.4. The quest to break the four-minute mile* (London, 2004), pp. ix–x.

[58] Bale, *Roger Bannister and the four-minute mile*, p. 137.

# The Four Minute Mythology: Documenting Drama on Film and Television

Garry Whannel

In 2004, on the 50th anniversary of the first sub-four minute mile, a group of scholars came together in Oxford to mark, discuss and analyse an event of a totally arbitrary character – the four-minute mark is a mere product of our segmentation of time and does not denote a significant barrier in any other way. This only serves to underline the immense power of the symbolic. In discussion of Bannister's four-minute mile the emphasis should be on interpretation and representation and not just 'fact', but when sports enthusiasts meet together they can often, after a convivial stirrup cup or two, embark on an energetic hunt for facts regardless of relevance or significance. Sport generates statistics and statistics produce statisticians. It is often the case that discussion of sport films becomes bogged down in the marshy ground of an ever more arcane comparison between the 'false' representation of the text and the 'real' facts of the event. Debates about *Chariots of Fire* were dogged by the tendency of some to judge the film harshly on the basis of its 'distortion' or altering of the facts. For example, the runner and devout Christian Eric Liddell did not, as the film suggests, discover at a late hour that his heats were to be run on a Sunday: he knew well in advance that this would be the case and changed his event accordingly. The secret manoeuvres depicted in the film were not necessary. These issues are, of course, important to air, and an understanding of history depends on a clear grasp of established events.

I do not think, though, that this has much bearing on a consideration of *Chariots of Fire* as a film. It is more worthwhile to examine the themes, structures and representational strategies through which the film works. I want to make clear at the outset that in offering some analytic comments about the television film *Four Minute Mile* my intention is to examine the themes and modes of representation of Bannister's four-minute mile and not to make any attempt to locate 'truth' or to compare filmic representation and reality. I do, however, want to precede discussion of the film with some comments on the social context of the race in which Bannister became the first man to run a mile in less than four minutes. More specifically, I want to outline the factors that led to its mythic status.

## Four-minute mythology

The breaking of the four-minute mile 'barrier' is one of the most heavily mythologized moments in British sporting history. In books, magazines, newsreels and television documentaries and on websites, it has become one of the signifiers of Britain in the 1950s. Many elements contribute to the emblematic nature of the 'moment' of Bannister's world record. These include:

a. As I have commented elsewhere, a sport event is not in itself a narrative. However, all sports events, in that they pose the question 'who will win?', are rooted in a structure that Roland Barthes called the hermeneutic code. [1] Hence they are available for narrativization, a concept that neatly describes what television does to sport. Sport events have a powerful hermeneutic structure that provides good strong dramatic potential. [2]
b. Among athletic events, the mile offers particularly good material for drama – it is neither too long nor too short; the story is easy to understand, the tactics simple enough to perceive and comprehend. The 100 metres can be spectacular, but is over in ten seconds: there is no real internal dramatic structure to a sprint. The 10,000 metres takes

too long: there are inevitably *longueurs* during which little narrative development takes place. Set against this is the fact that the mile is an Anglo-Saxon oddity in the metric world of athletics, and the fascination with the mile has been less strong on mainland Europe.

c. The throwing events and the long jump and triple jump are poorly structured from a dramatic point of view: the first performance in a competition can turn out to be the best. Only the pole vault and the high jump build towards a climax, but here the final act is always the failure of the final competitor to clear the bar.
d. Since 1945, the world record for the mile had been held by a Swede, Gunder Hägg, opening up the possibility of a British runner beating it, and so allowing for the development, in the UK, the USA and Australia, of a patriotic mobilization of interest.
e. Other foreign runners, such as Landy and Santee, were getting close to the four-minute barrier, thus heightening the dramatic tension and placing a positive (British) resolution in doubt.
f. The long period, since 1945, in which the record 'stalled' at 4 minutes 1.4 seconds, served to generate the 'mythology' of a barrier – a threshold that could not be crossed. Animated discussions as to whether the four minute mile was even possible were common.
g. This mythology was given symbolic force by the accidental drama of mathematics. The event, one mile, had to be performed in under four minutes, an average of less than one minute per lap. The prominence of the task in the popular imagination was boosted by the arbitrary significance of a numerical marker – four minutes – and from the neatness of relation between time and space (four laps, four minutes).
h. Finally, when the event was achieved, Norris McWhirter's famous announcement of the result added considerably to the dramatic appeal of the moment. McWhirter milked the moment for its drama, by announcing, in pedantic style, the winner, Roger Bannister, and then the succession of records broken, before finally revealing to the agog crowd, the time. To add to the drama, he was able to pronounce 'in a time of three . . .' the rest of his words being drowned out by the cheering crowd. Indeed the race itself, a planned and paced record attempt with only one valid contender was largely devoid of drama, with the exception of the invisible struggle of Bannister against the clock. In the film record of the event, the most dramatic visual moment is the collapse of Bannister after crossing the line and the cut to his exhausted face, seeming to signify the immensity of the task that has been performed.

The dramatic climax of the race itself was in turn the culmination of a competitive battle between athletes of several nations, ending in a British triumph, a world record, and a new athletic milestone.

To further strengthen the narrative potential for the film, Landy subsequently beat Bannister's record, and the year's athletic season was to culminate in Vancouver with the 1954 Empire Games, offering a showdown between the two. The social and historical context is also of some relevance. It happened in the twilight of empire and the dawn of television, amid post-war austerity. The 1954 Empire Games were the last one so named before it became the Empire and Commonwealth Games in 1958.

Television was still in its infancy – BBC's one television channel was eight years old, but was only just beginning to challenge radio's audiences. The programme *Sportsview,* at the very start of its long run, was able to feature film of Bannister's achievement. [3] Like Matthews's famous FA Cup Final the previous year, the Bannister four-minute mile is bound up with the birth of television sport. It looks utterly unlike the television events that we subsequently became familiar with. In black and white, it was shot on one film camera from a position that had a logic to it, but was at complete variance with the visual television grammar that was coming into being. The camera was, more or less, at ground level, and the view of the race is frequently obscured by figures standing between the camera and the track.

Yet the Bannister mile is more accessible to us than many great sporting accomplishments of just a few years earlier that were not even captured on film. Like the England v Hungary game, the winning of the Ashes by England in 1953 and the Matthews final, it is part of a threshold moment between the pre-televisual and the world of television sport that was being forged. Along with the Coronation, Hillary's ascent of Everest and Matthews's Cup Final medal, it was mobilized as part of a set of images of the post-war reconstruction of a post-empire Britain. Ever since, the image of Bannister crossing the line and collapsing has been part of the lexicon of signifiers of the 1950s.

As an event, I would also suggest that it marked another significant step on the road to professionalization, although it preceded the commercialization and commodification of sport from the 1960s. It is true that Bannister, now often portrayed as emblematic of the amateur era, trained part-time, continued his medical education as a doctor, adopted a light racing programme and had no regular coach. But he utilized organized pacemaking, embarked on a single-minded pursuit of the four-minute barrier, made relatively early use of precise interval training techniques and used Franz Stampfl as an advisor and mentor.

In this context he fits in a trajectory that links a figure such as Harold Abrahams in the 1920s (who used a professional coach and adopted a single-minded approach) Bannister in the 1950s, and Coe and Ovett (full-time athletes) in the 1970s and 1980s. A fellow contributor to this volume, John Hoberman, after a detailed study of contemporary evidence, raises interesting questions about the likelihood of Bannister's awareness of, if not use of, performance-enhancing drugs. Whatever the truth of this, Bannister's achievement does now seem, in more ways than one, the start of the modern era in athletics.

## *Four Minute Mile*: The film

*Four Minute Mile* (1988) was a made-for-television film, in two parts, the result of a co-production between BBC Television and ABC Australia. It tells the story of the race to become the first man to run a mile in under four minutes, and specifically the rivalry between John Landy and Roger Bannister. The term sport film is merely a descriptive one – it does not denote a distinct style or a genre, but rather a topic. Having said that, there are some thematic and structural features that tend to link sport films of diverse subject matter. The narrative structure of sport films typically involves one of three elements – triumph over adversity, winning respect or the rise and fall of a central figure. Some films operate across a combination of these elements. The hermeneutic provided by the structure of the sporting competition poses the question 'who will win?' while the conventions of mainstream narrative cinema mean that this is usually likely to be the main protagonist. An effortless victory constitutes a profoundly uninteresting story, and as there must be obstacles in the path of the hero, the triumph over adversity is a common structure. In doing so, the triumph sometimes involves the winning of respect rather than victory. In *Cool Runnings*, *Rocky* and *A League of Their Own*, the narratives revolve around the ways in which respect of fellow competitors can be gained. There are a set of common themes that typically appear in sport films. Class, often unacknowledged, often displaced, is nevertheless often the locus of tension between characters. Gender typically appears in the form of tension between men who are totally focused on sport and women who are marginalized. Work is a key theme, often in the form of the tension between a puritan work ethic and the temptations of hedonism. National identity is a frequent motif, often involving tensions between authority and individual.

The film *Four Minute Mile* traces a simple linear narrative from the 1952 Olympics to the 1954 Empire Games and in each part there are, in effect, three sections. Part one commences with the Helsinki Olympics in 1952, continues to trace the attempts of Landy and Santee and their impact on Bannister, and culminates with the Bannister-McWhirter arranged record attempt at Motspur Park and its subsequent non-ratification. Part Two commences with the training for and achieving of the sub-four-minute mile in Oxford, continues with Landy's world record and culminates with Bannister's triumph in Vancouver. The events of history were easily transformed into dramatic structure. The story lends itself well to narrativization. If the Oxford race lacks in dramatic tension, the announcement of the time compensates. The Vancouver race provides a perfect dramatic ending but only for a British audience. Herein lies the source of much of the internal tension of the film, which elevates it from a mere reflective rendition of events. As a multinational co-production, it was targeting different national viewing publics. Landy is presented as a more sympathetic character and audience identification with him is structured in. In this sense the film is addressing an Australian audience; and it is notable that it ends not with Bannister's victory in Vancouver, but with the presentation by the British team of a plaque to Landy at a subsequent banquet.

The contrast between Bannister and Landy is established from the start, and is a consistent theme throughout. Landy is shown as modest and friendly; Bannister as tight, arrogant, tetchy and cold. Landy has a fairly poor, but supportive, family; Bannister is shown as privileged but rather isolated and asexual, whereas Landy is portrayed as having an enthusiastic awareness of women. Landy does well running with a hangover and a breakfast of pies; Bannister is controlled and calculating. Bannister is shown as supercilious and sceptical: 'How does someone suddenly improve by eight seconds in six months?' he snaps when hearing of Landy's first 4 minutes 2 seconds result. Although the film nominally focuses on three runners vying for the record, Santee's role is rather more marginal, partly because he never raced against either Bannister or Landy, diminishing the opportunity for drama.

The apparent class basis for the Bannister/Landy contrast, though, is displaced on to an opposition between urban/rural. From the start, Landy is portrayed as a small-town boy – the mayor set up an appeal to raise money for him to attend Helsinki, while his parents contributed half. His fellow athlete Les recounts how in his town there was a rabbit drive and he raised the money by shooting 7,000 rabbits. Bannister moves between London and Oxford, his laboratory and medical research and the running track. His companions are urbane, upper-middle-class and sophisticated. In narrative terms, Landy's 'helper' is the Finland-based runner Johannsen, who transports him to an idyllic pastoral landscape in order to train intensively. Bannister's 'helper', Franz Stampfl, played in the film by Michael York, is laden with European cultural capital with hints of Vienna, the opera and psychology. Landy is in nature, rural and pastoral, while Bannister in culture and science. Bannister's one excursion into the countryside, prompted by Brasher's love of rock climbing, is presented as a break from routine, rather than a core part of his identity.

Undercover payments were not unknown in athletics in the 1950s, and common by the 1970s. The television era, the growth of the sports clothing market, spearheaded by Adidas, and the growth of commercial sponsorship brought new money into the sport and in the process sharpened the contradictions and hypocrisies of amateurism, which finally began to collapse in the 1980s. It would be very hard for a film about athletics made in the 1990s not to be partly about amateurism and professionalism. The issue never becomes prominent in *Four Minute Mile* but it is there as a half-developed subtext. Santee is suspended for accepting a camera and later exposes himself to suspension by commentating on a race. Santee is portrayed as having a chip on his shoulder about the lack of support for his personal aspirations, but from the Oxbridge perspective he is a privileged college athlete with a full-time professional coach. By contrast, Landy shows no sign of bitterness at his own lack of strong financial support. Bannister's rigged record attempt is not ratified, and Chataway is shown getting conned into commentating on a race. Bannister is shown as having a rather ungracious attitude to Chataway's helping Landy; and the famous moment in which he sharpens his spikes signifies his thorough, almost pedantic, preparation. So the ghost of professionalism, never quite made flesh, haunts the film. Landy does not feature within this subtext (one wonders what he lived on in Finland) and so appears as the bearer of the 'true' amateur spirit.

All three athletes allude to patriotism. In the case of Santee it is utilized as part of an attempt to persuade his coach to let him concentrate on the mile rather than the relay. Confronted with accusations that he is putting his own individual needs before loyalty to the team and the university, he counters that 'if we win the relay all the university will cheer; if I break four minutes, all of America will cheer'. So he evokes patriotism for individual motives. Bannister's desire for the record is placed in the context of British events that capture public attention. Bannister listens to news of the conquest of Everest and then, while the Coronation is on the television, rings Don McMillan to enlist his help in the record attempt with the words 'it would be a pity if an American got there first'. Bannister here is portrayed not so much as a patriotic subject as someone manipulating empire loyalties and anti-Americanism. So both Bannister and Santee appear to exploit patriotism rather than be caught up in it. By contrast, Landy's concerns are with failing to fulfil the expectations of his fellow citizens – he worries on the plane to Helsinki: 'I just hope I don't let them all down.'

Work features as a theme in terms of training and the contemporary debate within coaching circles about quantity versus intensity. Landy becomes persuaded of the efficacy of Czech runner Emil Zatopek's legendary high mileage training. After encountering him at Helsinki, Landy twice muses: 'We don't train hard enough.' In the absence of an Eastern bloc dimension, the Zatopek theme appears to stand for a Stakhanovite concept of work-rate. Santee represents a distinctively American individualized 'winning is everything' ethos, but is frustrated by the emphasis the coach places on running for the university. Bannister represents determination: at one point he comments 'I have to do something to make them eat their words' – echoing the declaration of Harold Abrahams in *Chariots of Fire* that 'I'm going to run them off their feet'. However, whereas for Abrahams 'they' were the tradition-bound university old guard, for Bannister 'they' are the iconoclastic British press.

In the film Bannister is shown as largely self-directed until the last few months when Stampfl's advice and guidance is accepted. If there is a case that Bannister has self-mythologized himself as the light trainer, and sought to mask the extensive and careful scientific preparation he undertook, then this film, like Bannister's autobiography *The first four minutes*, tends to reproduce that mythology. [4] In both, the role of Stampfl is somewhat minimized. Yet in the film, the figure of Stampfl, in another sense, is pivotal. The race took place in an era that is characteristically represented as one in which British sport was ruled by amateur gentlemen in blazers with brass buttons. An assumption of British superiority had yet to be dented. There was a disdain among the British sporting establishment for foreign methods and foreign coaches. Bannister's use of Stampfl went against the grain of the athletics establishment of the 1950s, of which Harold Abrahams was a key member. There is a conscious irony here since, as was famously depicted in *Chariots of Fire*, 30 years earlier Harold Abrahams himself employed a foreign coach, Sam Mussabini, whose presence exposed the combination of hostility to all matters professional and foreign among the Cambridge establishment, as represented by the college grandees. In *Four Minute Mile*, Abrahams has become the personification of a confidence in English superiority, soon to be thoroughly demolished by the growing post-war dominance of the Olympic Games by the USA and USSR, and by the football successes of Hungary. So Stampfl, as a shadowy Svengali, was the wave of the future even though it was to be another 40 years before foreign football managers began to dominate British football.

It is Oxford itself that is at the core of the mythology – derided in the film as the home of the gentleman amateur – and of 'effortless superiority'. Dennis Johannsen tells Landy that he refers to the Oxbridge athletes as 'the Achilles heels'. At the conclusion of part one, Bannister announces in rather pompous fashion to his team: 'Gentlemen, we have three months.' Of course Bannister's single-minded and calculated approach is set against this image of Oxbridge casual effortlessness – nowhere more so than in the schools meeting in June 1953, into which McWhirter and Bannister insert a staged race as a record attempt. In the film, it is Abrahams (played by Richard Wilson) who argues against ratification, another ironic nod towards *Chariots of Fire*, in which Abrahams, rather than a bastion of establishment tradition, is portrayed as the great rebel-modernizer!

It may seem curious that Bannister is the hero who triumphs, yet Landy is clearly presented throughout in a more sympathetic manner. He is modest, unassuming and friendly, where Bannister is cold and aloof. His humble roots and the pastoral context of his training contrast with the urban intensity of Bannister's preparation. Landy's patriotism is, unlike that of Bannister and Santee, not seen as inner-directed or self-serving. The clue is that this was a co-production and an Australian audience, deprived of the victor, needed to have the most sympathetic character as a figure of identification.

## Documentary-dramatized and drama-documented

*Four Minute Mile* is a realist drama-documentary. Of course there is not one single realism: the word denotes a large number of specifiable realisms in different media at different periods. The drama-documentary mode has developed a set of relatively coherent and consistent characteristics that can, taken together, be regarded as a specific style of realism. Realism, though, is a complex concept in that it embodies both a style and a claim. As a style, filmic realism typically minimizes the obtrusiveness of the filmic process and minimizes our awareness of the process of construction. It characteristically utilizes standard angles, 'natural' lighting, naturalistic dialogue, unobtrusive background music and naturalistic sound effects.

Realism asserts itself as a superior mode of apprehending the 'real'; penetrating to and revealing truth. In that drama-documentary combines a fictonalized reconstruction of events, appearances and dialogue with the reportage form of documentary, it pushes this claim further, in its implicit suggestion that 'this is how it was'. So as a form it has always tended to be controversial precisely in that it purports to claim: this is how it was, and tends to conceal its own point of view as unproblematic truth. To me the interesting issues arising from the mode of representation in *Four Minute Mile* are not so much to do with its adequacy to 'the truth' but rather in its mobilization of audience sympathies. It is easy to see how the same film, made for an American audience might have made Santee a more heroic character whose talents were thwarted, rather than as a spoiled brat who couldn't quite cut it. A different form of portrayal, even without dialogue changes could have made Bannister a more attractive character. In *Four Minute Mile* these strategies of positionality, identification and mode of address are embedded within and partially masked by the drama-documentary aesthetic style. Yet the entertainment value in *Four Minute Mile* seems higher than that of the recent somewhat pedestrian television documentary screened on BBC2 in April 2004. The facts, then, are not enough – as an audience we want access to the emotional intensities beneath the surface, even if a fictionalized level is the only way in which such 'access' can be offered.

I want to draw attention to a couple of similarities and differences with other filmic drama-documentary representations of British sport. First, there is an apparent structural regularity to do with the treatment of class. The displacement of class tensions onto an urban-rural contrast occurs in *Chariots of Fire*, when we first encounter Harold Abrahams arriving as a new undergraduate at his Cambridge college and singing Gilbert and Sullivan at the Freshers' Fair. We then meet Liddell in the pastoral setting of the Highland Games. Abrahams is an urban sophisticate with cultural capital, mingling with the elite; Liddell a good honest down-to-earth man amidst ordinary people. Similarly, if more dramatically, at the start of *Bodyline*, [5] the story of the 1932–3 English cricket tour of Australia, we meet Douglas Jardine, a child of the Empire and the Raj, surrounded by servants, meeting lords and swamped in privilege; and then meet Don Bradman in a small Australian town; like Liddell and Landy, framed in pastoral greenery. All three films, then, counterpose a privileged and intense bearer of cultural capital with a man of humble rural origins.

However, Oxbridge is by no means a static and fixed point in these representations. In *Chariots of Fire* Cambridge is briefly painted in a warm brown nostalgic glow, reminiscent of the early scenes of Oxford in the television adaptation of Evelyn Waugh's *Brideshead Revisited*, before being used to signify a tradition-bound reactionary and anti-Semitic institution that has to be forced to change. In *True Blue*, [6] by contrast, the amateur spirit of working together and respecting loyalty triumphs over a more brutish and ruthless American will to win at all costs. In *Four Minute Mile*, Oxbridge is neither the tradition-bound obstacle nor the source of a more noble ethos, but rather the backdrop and context in which friends come together and find a path. If Bannister has an obstacle against which he struggles, it is the abstraction of the four-minute barrier and the scepticism of the British press.

## The Bannister moment and the emergence of television

'Many of the dramatic events of the period – Bannister's four minute in 1954, Matthews' FA Cup Final of 1953, England winning the Ashes in 1953, Real Madrid's 7–3 European Cup Final victory in 1960 – were captured by the television cameras yet still seem part of a pre-televisual world.' [7]

Bannister's four-minute mile, like other events of that moment, were, it seems to me now, transitional moments in sport – situated on the liminal threshold of the television era. They are neither pre-televisual nor fully televisual, and were captured for us in modes that precede the formalization of television's visual grammar for sports coverage. [8] Since television sport reached its mature form around the start of the 1980s, the formal conventions have remained relatively constant. The containing of the live event within the show format, with its preview, intermediate discussion and post-mortem; the repetition of moments of peak excitement from multiple angles, at both normal speed and in slow motion; the post-action interviews – all are familiar and expected elements in the lexicon of television sport. The foregrounding of and celebration of the star performers seems unexceptional – a routinized element in the celebrity culture in which fashion, glamour, fitness, gossip, Hollywood cinema, lifestyle television and sports stadia converge. Indeed it is difficult to imagine the cultural form of sport before television became its defining medium. The four-minute mile of Roger Bannister had a presence on the television screen, yet was not a televised sporting moment in the way we now understand it. The technology was still very basic; routinized modes of coverage had yet to emerge; and the audience was small. Yet these moments provide clues, pointers, to the imminent and extraordinary growth of television sport.

Emergent media take a while to develop regularized cultural forms. The early uses of new media are often different from the forms that they later assume – one only needs to recall the early development of the Internet as a means for scientists to pool their data to illustrate this point. Audiences and audience practices have to be produced and routinized, and a regularizing of the relation between the production and consumption of a medium's product has to be established – we have to learn how to consume in a gradual process, involving technological refinement, state regulation, commercial investment and popular wants, needs and desires.

Raymond Williams outlined two models utilized to explain the development of media. The first, technological determinism, regards advance as driven by new technological innovation; the second regards technological innovation as symptomatic of social changes. Williams proposes a more complex model in which social change and technological innovation interact, and suggests restoring the notion of intent to conceptualization of technological development. [9] In analysing the relation of culture and technology in society, Castells argues that there is a 'historically articulated complex of transformations, which concerns simultaneously, capitalism as a social system, informationalism as a mode of development, and information technology as a powerful working instrument'. [10] These multi-factorial statements suggest ways to understand the growth of the technologies of television sport. The evolution of television sport was driven by the need to win audiences; the need to spectacularize sport; and hence the development of such devices as action replay, slow motion and, much later, tele-track. Our subsequent habituation to the presence of such devices contributes to the 'strange' and 'primitive' appearance of television sport in its emergent period.

In the formative period of television sport, the quality and hence 'realness' of the image was a key concern. Peter Dimmock, head of BBC Sport in the 1950s and 1960s, said the 'essence of a true "Outside Broadcast" is to report real happenings, while they happen and from where they happen'. [11] Much early innovation was associated with attempts to enhance this 'veracity' effect. Improvements to cameras and lenses made the image sharper, the introduction of colour enhanced its 'natural' character and video, action replay and slow motion provided the ability to recompose time.

By the mid-1970s, satellite-based telecommunications allowed the transmission and re-broadcast of live sport events around the globe. The technological ability to relay high-quality live images brought a new intimacy and closeness – that restructuring of cultural transactions that McLuhan famously dubbed 'the global village'. McLuhan's observation was prescient, although like any village it turns out to have a well entrenched social hierarchy in which there are those who are information-rich and information-poor. [12] Television sport has become the global village fete par excellence: the global reach of television, enabled by satellite technology, is part of a process in which 'flow' becomes more significant than 'space'. [13]

So if television sport was emerging as a distinct cultural form in the 1950s, how might one understand it? Stuart Hall has argued that television is a hybrid medium that borrowed and adapted its distinctive forms from other media, and thus evolved distinctive new forms – the magazine programme, the panel game, the sports broadcast. [14] Television took the basic sport event; simulated the view of an ideal spectator, added the ability to manipulate time, gave it an entertainment format with presenters and added the panel of experts, which combines intense seriousness with male bar-room camaraderie. Television felt its way tentatively at first and then with increasing confidence towards a routinized and conventionalized format. So *Television Sport Magazine* gave way to *Sportsview*, and irregular Saturday outside broadcasts spawned *Grandstand* (which ran from 1958 until its abrupt scrapping in 2006). In America, ABC came up with the influential *Wide World of Sports*, with its guiding principles 'up close and personal' and 'the thrill of victory, the agony of defeat'. [15]

Events such as Bannister's four-minute mile have a particularity born out of their temporal location in relation to television as a social institution. They are not really fully of the television age: captured by the cameras before the establishment of firm conventions of sport coverage, and before the technological maturation of the medium, they appear strange in their black-and-white graininess. Neither are they truly pre-televisual: they at least exist in televisual form – indeed their very graininess distinguishes them from earlier moments preserved on newsreel film or in photographs.

In the early days of television there was an uncertainty about the process of promoting and selling programmes to an audience. The *Radio Times* entries are characterized by a prosaic factual accuracy with little attempt to promote the programmes or win audiences. In addition, the content of sport programmes was sometimes unclear when *Radio Times* went to press. The European Cup Final of 1960 does not appear in the advance listings. On the evening Bannister broke the four-minute barrier, film of the race was shown in *Sportsview*, first launched a month earlier. The *Radio Times* entry, though, merely states, in low key fashion:

May 6 1954 . . .
**8.20 Sportsview**
Introduced by Peter Dimmock
Bringing to you from around the world of sport the latest news, views and personalities
Edited by Paul Fox
Presented by Dennis Monger

The Coronation in 1953 was the first event that put television centre stage as a major medium, although in the UK it took the launch of independent television in 1955 to really make the television audience grow. During the 1950s, sport was not really a big factor in the growth of the television audience – only from the time of the 1966 World Cup and then with the introduction of colour, action replay, slow motion and live satellite feeds does sport begin to become a more important factor in the appeal of TV.

This is not to deny the cultural centrality and significance of the broadcasting of major regular sporting events. Cardiff and Scannell argue that radio helped produce shared national corporate rituals: the Queen's Christmas Message and other royal occasions but also the Derby, the Grand National, the Boat Race and Cup Final Day. [16] Television built on and extended this sense of a significant proportion of the nation sitting down at the same moment to consume the same images. A period was inaugurated in which people shared the experience of being an audience, an experience typically marked in conversations at the workplace, at school gates and in shop queues about the previous night's television. This form of cultural exchange eventually became dubbed 'water-cooler' moments. In the deregulated, digitalized multi-channel era, sport is one of the few cultural forms left that regularly provides such moments.

The technological maturation of television, with live colour pictures from around the world, 'up close and personal' images with big close ups, was an important stage in the generation of a celebrity culture and subsequent commodification of the star image. First because the 'up close and personal' high-quality close-ups produce identification; and second because they produce familiarization with key stars. The constant compression of the story into key iconic moments, in highlights, capsule great moments, end sequences and title sequences, combined with the production of metonymic images in the press and magazines, mean that there is a routinized reduction of events to a single iconic moment (e.g. Gazza's tears). Bannister's four-minute mile, for example, is almost always represented by his crossing the finishing line and then breasting the tape. It is hard, however, for moments to emerge as iconic without the close-up and its endless replication across media. Examination of star pictures over the last 30 years suggests a growing self-consciousness of the mythologization process: witness for example the prevalence among footballers of trademark modes of celebration – signature poses.

Television, developing from its grainy black-and-white childhood into a colourful and sophisticated maturity as a medium, appears now to have entered a late middle age in which it exhibits a growing tendency to live not in the past but off its past. List programmes, nostalgia television – where are they now, who were they then? – are among the many pretexts for archive clip-based television. In part of course, this is driven by the economic need to find cheap ways of living off the back catalogue. Short clips do not involve the complex apparatus of rights clearance and repeat fees that full-scale repeats do. It is also a significant part of the popular culture equivalent of that process that Raymond Williams dubbed the 'selective tradition'. [17] Television's periodic capsule reviews of the history of sport mark a constant setting in place of performer, event and significance. [18] The past is constantly being reconstructed in the present.

Transformations in modes of news and sport presentation have an influence on the representation of history. Watching the video versions of England v Hungary 1954 and Real Madrid v Eintracht Frankfurt, and the film record of Bannister's four-minute mile, and reading the contemporary press coverage highlights the dramatic changes in the nature of sport coverage. There is now far more dramatization, personalization and sensationalism. The dominant impression of the coverage of these events is how low key it was by comparison with now. There was negligible build-up in advance and precious little fuss afterwards.

Even though it was the first Cup Final to be televised, the much mythologized Matthews final was given a low-key build-up in *Radio Times*. Just 13 years later, the World Cup got far more space and more hyperbole. Even this major event, however, disappeared from the newspapers a couple of days after the final. Bannister's four-minute mile was not mentioned in *The Times* until the middle column of page 8 and then with the distinctly low key headline:

> 4-MINUTE MILE
> TRIUMPH OF R.G. BANNISTER
> POOR CONDITIONS OVERCOME [19]

The reified and mythologized place some sport events occupy in accounts of the past can mislead us as to the degree of public attention that they won at the time. Thanks to television, 'the past' and 'black-and-white' are now firmly locked together. Modern drama, in attempting to represent the past, sometimes resorts to a simulated sepia and use of de-emphasized primary colours to reproduce a sense of the past. Accent, too, is utilized as connoting the past: BBC voices from the 1950s and earlier often sound so impossibly plummy to modern ears that they are ripe for satire. A marked division now hangs between the 1980s, when television had become a mature technology, and everything that came before, which, to young people, has become 'the olden days'. The 50th anniversary celebrations of Bannister's mile reminded us that such events have an extensive mythological potency. Yet we must remember that it is also possible for stars and events to fade from popular memory – at least one person to whom I mentioned this paper had never heard of Roger Bannister, and I feel confident that Sir Edmund Hilary, Stirling Moss and even Stanley Matthews do not inspire a light in the eye of many people under 40. It maybe that the image 'Bannister', apparently so iconic to the generation who grew up with television, is being rapidly borne back into the past.

## Notes

[1] Roland Barthes, *S/Z* (London, 1974).

[2] Garry Whannel, *Fields in vision: Television sport and cultural transformation* (London, 1992).

[3] Whannel, *Fields in vision*; Garry Whannel, 'Televising sport: The archaeology of a professional practice', in *Leisure, politics, planning, people, the media and cultural art forms*, 5 (Brighton, 1989).

[4] Roger Bannister, *The first four minutes* (London, 1955).

[5] *Bodyline*, (1984), Television mini series produced by Kennedy Miller Productions and Network 10, Australia.

[6] *True Blue*, (1996), Film produced by Booker Entertainment, Channel Four Films, Film and General Productions and Rafford Films.

[7] Garry Whannel, *Media sports stars, masculinities and moralities* (London, 2002).

[8] Garry Whannel, 'Pregnant with Anticipation: The Pre-History of Television Sport and the Politics of Recycling and Preservation', *International Journal of Cultural Studies, 8*, 4 (2005), pp. 405–426.

[9] Raymond Williams, *TV technology and cultural form* (London, 1974), pp. 9–32.

[10] Manuel Castells, *The informational city* (Oxford, 1989).

[11] Peter Dimmock, 'Television outside broadcasts', BBC lunchtime lecture, 2 Oct. 1968, p. 3 (London, 1968).

[12] Marshall McLuhan, *Understanding media* (London, 1964).

[13] Castells, *The informational city*.

[14] Stuart Hall, *TV as a medium and its relation to culture* (CCCS paper) (Birmingham, 1975).
[15] Garry Whannel, 'Grandstand, the sports fan and the family audience', in J. Corner, ed., *Popular television in Britain: studies in cultural history* (London, 1991).
[16] David Cardiff and Paddy Scannel, *The social foundations of British broadcasting* (London, 1981).
[17] Raymond Williams, *The long revolution* (London, 1961).
[18] Garry Whannel, 'History is being made: Television sport and their selective tradition', in R. Jackson and T. McPhail, eds., *The Olympic movement and the mass media* (Calgary, 1989).
[19] *The Times* (London), 7 May 1954.

# Inhibiting Progress: The Record of the Four-Minute Mile

Jim Denison

In this paper I explore the long-standing significance of the four-minute mile in line with the meaning it still holds today. A meaning, I will argue, that derives from the construction of an idealized past. To support my argument I will first discuss the concept of nostalgia, followed by an examination of how four minutes as a meaningful barrier first arose. Then, to demonstrate the ongoing significance of a sub-four-minute mile despite its almost meaningless stature in the world of international middle-distance running, I will cite material from interviews I conducted with six recent sub-four-minute milers. [1]

## Nostalgia

Even in today's metric age, the challenge of a sub-four-minute mile continues to inspire young runners and excite sport fans as an athletic standard known the world over. The time, 3:59, is a stamp of approval; it is something people know they can trust, a label or a brand that is safe and comforting. However, by the standards of a rational, decimal-based numerical system, the mile is a thing of the past, a nostalgic exhibition event that has no place in the metrics of the Olympic Games. Yet the mile continues to fascinate contemporary middle-distance runners, a generation, according to John Allemang, 'that is supposed to be hostile to the dusty glow of baby-boom memories'. [2] Reid Coolsaet, for example, a promising Canadian runner, dreams of breaking four minutes for a mile. 'I'd much rather run a 3:59 mile than a 3:41 1,500 metres. It shouldn't matter to me at all – I know they're the exact equivalent. But the reality is, I want the cachet of the mile.' [3]

It is in this way, then, that contemporary milers hold on to the past to interpret their present running goals and ambitions. As a result, nostalgia must be seen as more than an individual's innocent longing for the past. Frank Davis, for example, characterizes nostalgia as a memory of the past that is 'infused with imputations of past beauty, pleasure, and joy'. [4] Accordingly, people have an affection for the mile, a warm spot they maintain that derives from recollections of quality and goodness. Moreover, nostalgia is 'a deeply felt social emotion' [5] that impacts on our present and future understandings. However, nostalgia often brings with it a touch of sadness, because the very pleasure one perceives comes from a past age that cannot be relived in the present or the future. Of course the physical act of running a 3:59 mile can be relived again and again, but its relevance as a world-class performance will never return.

Pirkko Markula has specifically written about nostalgia's melancholy side with respect to various types of ethnic and cultural performances. She comments how the power of nostalgia prevents us from allowing people and cultures to change. 'We long for lost traditions when we attend cultural performances. We don't want to accept modern variations like neon colours in Native Americans' costumes, or ballet moves distracting the flow of flamenco. We want to witness what once was; what we have defined as "authentic" heritage.'[6]

Apparently we practise such dominating preservation techniques, according to Jean Baudrillard, because of the meaninglessness we experience in the present and our desire to restore some sense of purpose to our lives. [7] This longingness, for Baudrillard, is necessarily melancholy because we try to bring back what we have lost in the past – an imagined, idealized past – in order to survive or feel more worthwhile today. And quite often our way of connecting with the past is through the spectacle of performance. In this sense, Markula explains, citing Paul Connerton, 'performances such as sport have an important role to play in the persistence of our unconscious collective memory'. [8]

As numerous sports scholars have pointed out, nowhere in sport is the perpetuation of a specific memory enacted more overtly than in the opening ceremonies for events such as the Olympic Games and the Commonwealth Games. [9] For example, an integral part of these festivities is the display of traditional dances by the host country's indigenous people. These productions have led Markula to ask: 'Through these performances do we demonstrate our respect for native peoples, or our respect for the stereotypical image of them that we have created?' [10]

Similarly, regarding the celebrations that took place on 6 May 2004 to commemorate the 50th anniversary of the first four-minute mile, including a re-enactment of the race, can't we ask ourselves: 'Are we really recognizing Roger Bannister's achievement in its own right, or are we instead expressing our desire to return to some bygone era of athletics?' But curiously there is no authentic athletics era from the past for us to return to. And would the majority of today's athletes really want to go back to those days and run on cinder tracks in poor shoes for no money? Although, in a bizarre case of retro-running, a high school in Cambridge, Ontario, had its synthetic track dug up and replaced with a 'Bannister-era' surface made out of crushed brick and clay in order to hold a throwback day of mile races and give running a four-minute mile 'meaning again', according to the race organizer, John Carson. [11] Just the same, the era of the four-minute mile is a constructed one, a history that was created for us by previous generations of milers, coaches, scientists and journalists that over time has been fashioned into athletics' golden age. Evidence of how this constructed past arose can be seen from the following brief history of the four-minute mile.

## The construction of sub-four

Since records in track and field were first set down in England in 1860, the mile has survived as one of the sport's premier events. Through the late nineteenth and early twentieth centuries, great sportsmen across Europe and America sought their fame and fortune as milers: Walter George, Paavo Nurmi, Glenn Cunningham. Bookmakers, too, seized on the public's fascination with the mile and believed, as they did with boxing, that miling could capture people's emotions and garner a wager.

As the mile world record fell from 4:55 in 1861 to 4:18 in 1884, and to 4:12 in 1915, talk quickly turned to the possibility of a mile in under four minutes. The English coach Walter Harrington asserted in 1921:

'Times are dropping . . . men are strengthening . . . soon no barrier, even four minutes, will hold milers prisoner.' [12] The American impresario Asa Bushnell, who organized grand mile invitationals at Princeton University in the early 1930s, [13] believed that packed stadiums, international rivalries and man's undying curiosity 'to see the other side' would quickly bring about a four-minute mile.

The mile's progression has always been a talking point – from the great rivalry between Sebastian Coe and Steve Ovett, which saw the world record lowered an astonishing three times in just 18 days in 1981 and reported daily on the front page of the *New York Times*, to banner headlines announcing new mile records in *The Times* of London 100 years earlier. And across towns and villages in America and Britain where a four-minute mile has never been run, local promoters attempt to create this spectacle as a way of anointing 'their place' a legitimate track and field town.

Despite the mile's elimination from major championships in favour of the 1,500 metres, it remains current and contemporary: meet organizers today still include it on their programmes – Oslo's Dream Mile, Rome's Golden Mile, Britain's Emsley Carr Mile; fans and journalists anticipate faster times yet, and statisticians continue to chart the year's top 50 performances.

Officially, however, it was not until 1933, when the New Zealander Jack Lovelock ran 4:07.6 to set a new mile world record that the term 'four-minute mile' was coined by a *New York Herald* sports reporter. [14] In the next ten years, however, Lovelock's world record fell by only 1.6 seconds, prompting leading sports commentators to speculate that there must be some kind of 'wall' at four minutes. But then in 1943 Sweden's Arne Anderson produced a stunning 4:02.6, followed the next year by 4:01.6. And later that same year his countryman Gunder Hägg ran 4:01.4. 'Surely a breakthrough was near,' clamoured the sporting press. 'Whatever mysteries lay on the other side of four minutes were bound to be discovered.' [15]

But the Swedes' progress stalled and Hägg's record remained intact for ten years. This prompted leading scientists, doctors and coaches to speculate on whether four minutes was humanly possible. Writing about this period in sport, Frank Deford of *Sports Illustrated* said: 'The poles had been reached, the mouth of the Nile found, the deepest oceans marked, the tallest mountain scaled, and the wildest jungles trekked but the distance of ground that measured a mile continued to resist all efforts to traverse it, on foot, in less than four minutes.' [16]

Whoever broke four minutes first, therefore, would achieve a heroic feat and establish himself as the boldest explorer of his time. Thus, entering the 1950s, 4:00.0 became a symbolic figure and its quest essential to our mythology. Interestingly, more than 50 years on and this is still the case, as contemporary milers' understandings of what represents a meaningful mile time continues to reflect this nostalgic construction. As evidence of this, I would like to present some results from a series of interviews I carried out with six contemporary milers, all of whom ran their first sub-four-minute mile after 1986 – more than 30 years after Bannister did it for the first time. In each case my subjects spoke reverentially about the enduring meaning that breaking four minutes for a mile has held in their lives.

## A lasting standard

When Michael East, Britain's current number one miler, first broke four minutes on 22 July 2001, his reaction was a curious mixture of the past's significance which allowed him to rationalize and fashion the present into something much more satisfying. 'When I did it I was like, Oh wow, that's excellent. And even though I finished last in the race I ended up getting the result sheet with my name and time on it framed. It's now on the wall in my lounge.' [17] Would an athlete in any other event feel so good about finishing last?

Or consider the reaction of Irish miler Desmond English, who first ran under four minutes on 25 June 1994:

> That sub-four made me feel like the fifteen years I had put into training and racing, and all the sacrifices I had made finally paid off. It justified everything I had done in my track life up to that point. In my own mind, breaking four gave me a key to this exclusive club that I had never imagined myself capable of entering, and that was just so thrilling. [18]

But there is no society of sub-four-minute milers. Today a sub-four-minute mile won't even earn a runner an invitation to any of the dozens of grand prix track meets held each summer across Europe and other parts of the world. The positive sense of achievement that English and other milers feel from breaking four minutes is more likely to be some form of private nostalgia stemming from their own subjective meanings regarding the significance of breaking four minutes. But private meanings located in the present, of course, largely depend upon our knowledge of the past. And this past knowledge, Connerton explains, 'tends to be shaped by various recollected images that are conveyed and sustained in the present'. [19] For example, who can forget the famous photograph of Bannister crossing the line after his 3:59.4 and collapsing into the arms of his Oxford chums? We are left with the image of a wall or some other type of barrier that exists at four minutes – a barrier that requires untold courage and strength to cross. Stepping over the finish line in a mile race before the clock reaches four minutes has become synonymous with reaching the top of an unexplored mountain peak, or stepping across a hazardous border. It holds the weight of a heroic conquest.

But the line across the track at four minutes is something arbitrary. It is simply how athletics has been mapped in the West. And as ridiculous as it is that tourists who travel by plane to the North Pole receive a certificate for crossing the Artic Circle, it is equally ridiculous for present-day runners who compete on all-weather tracks with a full-time diet of training to think that breaking four minutes is something remarkable. Yet the fact is that they do.

American Dan Wilson, for example, was so impressed with himself after he ran his first sub-four-minute mile on 4 February 2001 that he reorganized his life. With his parents' blessing, he quit his job, doubled his training mileage and moved to a remote town in North Carolina to prepare without distraction for what he believed would be the next phase in his running career: the Olympics, a string of invitations to race around the world. [20]

Clearly four minutes is somehow part of our common consciousness or curriculum, particularly in Britain and America. It is general knowledge, or something we absorb – 'four minutes for a mile' – as part of our shared or collective memory. The four-minute mile represents this lasting but also contemporary benchmark that we immediately associate with athletics and with running. Most people across the English speaking world still think that four minutes remains *the* standard for the mile. They aren't aware that it is now something much faster, or that the world record for the mile is down to 3:43.

Even Kenyan middle-distance runners, who are all raised on metrics, develop an appreciation for the value of breaking four minutes when they reach an international standard and leave Kenya to race in Europe or America. Joseph Chesire, for example, a top Kenyan athlete in the late 1980s, told William Tanui just as his international career was beginning in the early 1990s, 'Break four minutes when you run the mile. Then according to the English people you are not a bad runner.' [21] The world's second fastest miler of all time, Kenyan Noah Ngeny, expressed a similar sentiment:

> In my first race outside Kenya I ran a mile in Scotland. It was a distance I had never heard of before. My time was 4:01 and I didn't know what that meant – if it was good or bad. But then I was told that it's good to break four minutes. And so that became my goal. And the next time I ran the mile I did much better. I ran 3:50.41. I was very pleased that now I could be considered a real miler and a good athlete because I had broken four minutes. [22]

It is in this way, therefore, that a runner can create a respectable sporting identity by breaking four minutes. But a 3:59 mile is a unique athletic achievement because despite its mediocre standing on any sort of annual world list, its cultural capital both inside and outside athletics circles remains high.

Martin Hemsley, for example, an American who broke four minutes only once, on 17 May 1986, commented on how he confronts the mystique of four minutes all the time in business:

> Somehow people find out that I ran a sub-four-minute mile and then they ask me about it. It's uncomfortable for me when people bring it up because they don't know how four minutes fits into the larger scheme of track. They think because I broke four minutes I must have run in the Olympics and been some super star when it's really not that way at all. [23]

As a barrier, therefore, four minutes continues to carry with it tremendous respect despite its mediocre standing. It is seen as a general human endeavour that transcends borders and nationalities, like climbing Mount Everest. But interestingly, beside a few exceptions, the mile remains largely invisible on the present international racing landscape, replaced as it has been at all major championships by the 1,500 metres. As a result, the mile has turned into something that is spoken about or imagined more than it is seen. The lore and mystery around Roger Bannister survives in most people's minds as to what world-class middle-distance running is today. A fast 1,500 metres isn't something the average sports fan can appreciate. And it is unlikely that 3:33 or 3:31 for 1,500 metres will ever replace the existing categories of 'running excellence' that people carry around in their heads.

To explain how it is that we perpetuate the superiority of a 3:59 mile, Baudrillard would say that in these postmodern times images have become more real for us than the actual world we live in. [24] Standards, expectations, quality – these are all marked today for us by images that precede the real. Society, then, or more specifically the world of elite middle-distance running, is hyperreal, where the world record for the mile, 3:43, is devoid of meaning. In this respect, 3:43 has become a transparent achievement for milers today. And Baudrillard would say that its meaninglessness makes runners' lives today empty, which is why so many young runners look back to the past to restore what is more meaningful to them: a 3:59 mile.

Moreover, we are also uncomfortable with how the standard of excellent middle-distance running has moved far away from our shores. Previous systems of domination that the West maintained in sport, such as amateurism and colonialism, have been dismantled. Middle-distance running today is professional not amateur, and it is African not European or American. The effect of this transformation can be seen in the poor quality of the West's current stable of middle-distance runners. So what are young middle-distance runners left to strive for today? If the results of my interviews are anything to go by, it is some sort of connection to the past in order to interpret the present more favourably: a present where they can feel good about themselves by achieving a mark that still has the cachet of immortality – namely by running a 3:59 mile.

## Conclusion

As middle-distance running standards continue to deteriorate in the West, we are left to celebrate the past – times such as the 1950s, when milers from America, Australia and Europe were the best in the world. This serves to distract us from the present and from a future that we do not want to face. Losing one's traditions hurts, but perpetuating the relevance of a four-minute mile allows us to feel good. Further, we protect our fantasies surrounding the worth of four minutes by fashioning inaccurate ideas of African running that are based on stereotypes only. African runners' success, we tell ourselves, is genetic or particular to their high-altitude upbringing. We deny the fact that these former colonial nations of ours have changed, and that our relationship with them must change too.

It is here, therefore, where nostalgia begins to be shaped by power relations as we fail to see how our Western constructions of Africa's running culture actually perpetuate the idea of Western superiority. We celebrate Roger Bannister as a great explorer who practised sport the 'right way'; we have trouble accepting the progress made in running by other nations and as a result we continue to look back on the past in an idealized, sentimentalized way. As a consequence we stifle our own development and our progress ceases. Thus, contemporary runners' fixation with four minutes for a mile can potentially serve to inhibit the development of middle-distance running in Europe and America. Subsequently, a new breed of runner is emerging in the West who is more concerned with tradition than forging ahead to create a new future.

## Notes

[1] These interviews are from Jim Denison, *Bannister and beyond: The mystique of the four-minute mile* (Halcottsville, NY, 2003).
[2] John Allemang, 'Magnificent obsession: The four-minute mystique', *Globe and Mail* (Toronto), 1 May 2004, p. 25.
[3] Ibid., p. 26.
[4] Frank Davis, *Yearning for yesterday* (New York, 1979), p. 14.
[5] Ibid., p. viii
[6] Pirkko Markula, 'Dancing with postmodernism', *Waikato Journal of Education*, 3 (1988), p. 77.
[7] Jean Baudrillard, *Simulations* (New York, 1983).
[8] Paul Connerton, *How societies remember* (Cambridge, 1989).
[9] Robert Rinehart, *Players all: Performances in contemporary sport* (Bloomington, IN, 1988), Synthia Sydnor, 'Burning desire: Nostalgia, Ritual and the sport-festival flame ceremony', *Sociology of Sport Journal*, 8 (1991).
[10] Markula, 'Dancing with postmodernism', p. 78.
[11] Allemang, 'Magnificent obsession', p. 26.
[12] James McNeish, *Lovelock* (Auckland, 1994), p. 35.
[13] Ibid., p. 56.
[14] Ibid., p. 98.
[15] Ibid., p. 18.
[16] Frank Deford, 'Pioneer miler Roger Bannister and Everest conqueror Edmund Hillary became, at midcentury, the last great heroes in an era of sea change in sport', *Sports Illustrated*, 27 Dec. 1999, p. 105.
[17] Denison, Bannister and beyond, p. 246.
[18] Ibid., p. 204.
[19] Connerton, How societies remember.
[20] Denison, Bannister and beyond, p. 246.
[21] Ibid., p. 191.
[22] Ibid., p. 220.
[23] Ibid., p. 187.
[24] Baudrillard, *Simulations*.

# Amphetamine and the Four-Minute Mile

John Hoberman

On 6 June 1957, a front-page story in the *New York Times* reported on a startling theory that had been put forward by Dr Herbert Berger, an expert on drug addiction and a consultant to the United States Public Health Service. Speaking at the annual meeting of the American Medical Association at the Waldorf-Astoria Hotel in Manhattan, Dr Berger had suggested that it was amphetamine, the stimulant sold under the trade name of Benzedrine, that had made it possible for athletes to run the mile in less than four minutes. 'When I was a college boy,' Dr. Berger remarked, 'the four-minute mile was as unlikely as flying to the moon'. [1] Although he did not direct accusations at individual athletes, Dr Berger found it odd that so many runners had broken the four-minute barrier in so short a period of time. It appeared that these men had been 'turned temporarily into super-athletes by the use of drugs'. [2] The first runner to have accomplished this feat was the British medical student Roger Bannister, who ran a mile in 3:59.4 seconds on 6 May 1954. During the three years that had elapsed since this historic event, the four-minute barrier had been breached 18 times by a total of 12 athletes around the world.

In the wake of Berger's provocative suggestion, several of these men issued categorical denials that they had ever used drugs (or ever would use drugs) to become faster runners. The American miler Don Bowden, who a week earlier had become the first American to run under four minutes, called Berger's remark 'a ridiculous and silly accusation'. Merv Lincoln of Australia stated that he took no drugs whatsoever and commented: 'It wouldn't be necessary.' [3] The Irish runner Ron Delany declared:

> The whole idea [that drugs are being used] is absurd and crazy. I have never used drugs to help me run and I don't know of anyone else who has, anywhere in the world. That includes all the four-minute milers. Track and field is an amateur sport – a clean sport. I don't think anyone in it would want to pay such a price just to win a race or break a record.

'I would never dream of using drugs,' Don Bowden said. 'All the coaches and athletes I know have too much integrity to use drugs.' [4] 'I know most of the great milers,' Bowden stated on another occasion. 'Using drugs would be beneath their dignity.' [5] Dr Roger Bannister, the most famous of these athletes, categorically denied any knowledge of drug use. 'I have heard nothing about the use of stimulants and I do not believe the charge,' he declared to *The New York Times*. [6] 'No runner of my acquaintance ever used stimulants,' he told *Newsweek*. [7]

To these denials and protests were added those of sports officials on both sides of the Atlantic. Daniel J. Ferris of the American Amateur Athletic Union stated that both his organization and the International Amateur Athletic Federation, the world governing body for track and field, 'had rules providing that anyone discovered taking drugs of any kind was subject to suspension for life'. [8] (It would be of great interest to know exactly when and why such rules were introduced.) The executive director of the National Collegiate Athletic Association 'said he knew of no such instances [of doping] and was certain that no responsible athletic department would permit the use of drugs'. [9] The National Collegiate Track Coaches Association passed a resolution condemning

> the unwarranted and unsubstantiated statements of Dr Ernest [*sic*] Berger made at the recent American Medical Association (AMA) meeting in New York. He attributes the development in track and field athletics to the indiscriminate use of harmful drugs, specifically compounds of benzedrine. We who are connected with track know that this statement is contrary to fact. [10]

Other protests were heard from the executive director of the United States Olympic Committee, members of the New York State Athletic Commission, and many high-school and college coaches. [11] In Britain, Sir Adolphe Abrahams, honorary medical officer to the International Athletic Board and British Olympic team, confidently declared that the four-minute mile 'owes nothing to amphetamine (or any other drug)'. [12]

This wave of indignant denials was also directed at Berger's larger claim that the use of stimulants was widespread in both amateur and professional sports in the United States. As the chairman of the New York State Medical Society's committee on narcotics and alcohol addiction, Berger was said to have presented evidence of such use that is not described in the contemporary accounts of his report. What we do know is that his testimony caused real consternation among his medical colleagues. The New York delegation at the AMA meeting offered a resolution on the use of stimulants in sports, warning that 'the indiscriminate administration of these stimulants or their use under the direction of nonmedical persons be condemned as dangerous to our youth'. The chairman of the Connecticut delegation described 'testimony painting a shocking picture of widespread and indiscriminate use of stimulants, such as amphetamine, to improve the performance of athletes in competition. It was said that this vicious practice extends to children in our schools.' [13]

These comments make it clear that objections to performance-enhancing drugs were being couched in language traditionally reserved for narcotics and the depravity that was assumed to accompany drug addiction. 'A drug addict,' *The Lancet* commented in 1937, 'suggests to many a vicious and rather disgusting person who, however wretched his condition may be, has brought it upon his own head.' [14] The conflation of athletic cheating and self-destructive moral depravity has been a permanent feature of the age of doping. Condemnations of doping during the twentieth century almost always relied on a mutually reinforcing combination of ethical and medical arguments that was inherently unstable because it required a 'doping' drug to violate both norms. This requirement, which originated in social norms external to sport, introduced instability into the definition of doping in two ways. First, a performance-enhancing drug without harmful side-effects would meet the criteria for medical safety and should therefore escape censure; similarly, an agreement among competing athletes to use the same drug would appear to make its use fair. In fact, uncertainty about the immorality of performance-enhancing drugs was evident during the 1950s, as we shall soon see. But the more prominent effect of the amphetamine controversy was to focus attention on both ethical and medical arguments on behalf of drug-free sport. The amphetamine controversy of the late 1950s thus served as a precursor to the doping controversies that would eventually engulf Olympic sport once anabolic steroids and blood-boosting drugs changed the dynamics of entire athletic disciplines such as weightlifting, cycling and throwing events for both men and women.

The public discussion that followed Berger's sensational amphetamine accusation thus raised fundamental questions about the high-performance sport culture that was emerging as the age of doping began in earnest during the 1960s. For example, Dr Berger's suspicions originated in the naive assumption that the four-minute milers had dramatically exceeded inherent human limits. In so doing he managed to overlook the fact that an entire generation had elapsed since he had imagined in college that running a four-minute mile was like 'flying to the moon'. Berger may also have been the first commentator whose scepticism about record-breaking became a major news story. With the benefit of hindsight, such scepticism now looks prescient and is taken for granted by many experts. Record performances regularly excite suspicion in societies that use many drugs that are also available to athletes.

Other topics that emerged during the amphetamine controversy demonstrate how the 1950s were in some ways an age of innocence that had not yet encountered the consequences of effective performance-enhancing drugs. The Australian runner's assertion that drugs simply 'wouldn't be necessary' to break records is a case in point. Another example of this innocence was Ron Delany's assumption that no one 'would want to pay such a price just to win a race or break a record'. Whether the exorbitant price to which he refers was of a medical or moral nature is an important question that is left unclear; he may, in fact, have been referring to both kinds of danger to the sportsman. And it is Delany who asserts that elite running was at this time 'an amateur sport – a clean sport'. The doping practices of the professional cyclists who competed across the English Channel in France were often ignored in the early discussions of doping, because they belonged to a different social world. [15] These responses to the amphetamine episode of 1957 evoke a simpler age that appears to have been unaffected by the idea that drugs might boost athletic performance.

This essay argues that we should not take this apparent innocence at face value. Indeed, within days of all those vehement denials, a different picture regarding drugs and athletes had begun to emerge. It turned out that 'pep pills' were, in fact, being used by athletes in the United States, Canada and Australia. The team physician of the Ottawa Rough Riders of the Canadian Football League, for example, reported that players on all the major Canadian football teams were using 'pep pills'. [16] But what were they saying about drugs and athletes in England, the home of the first of the four-minute miler? The answer to this question takes us beyond the small circle of elite milers, beyond the early British sports medical scene of the 1950s, and into a society in which amphetamine drugs were both plentiful and available to any adult who cared to buy them.

One of the more striking comments made during the 1957 controversy was Roger Bannister's assertion that he had 'heard nothing about the use of stimulants' by runners. If anyone was in a position to have heard about the use of drugs by athletes by 1957, it should have been the newly trained physician whose career as one of the world's premier middle-distance runners had concluded only a few years earlier. Bannister's interest in what is now called exercise physiology was well known at this time. As a medical student in the early 1950s he had done research at Oxford, 'conducting experiments in which subjects breathing different gas mixtures ran on a motor-driven treadmill at different speeds and gradients'. 'I began,' he wrote in 1955, 'to prepare my training programme and to test my physical reactions with the same precision that I had learnt in the laboratory.' [17] In September 1953 he spoke on the physiology of athletic training at the annual meeting of the British Association for the Advancement of Science. [18] In April 1955 he addressed the Harveian Society of London on the same topic. [19] Even as Dr Berger's amphetamine charges were echoing back and forth across the Atlantic, Bannister was publishing sports columns in the *Sunday Times*. [20] In October 1958 the *Journal of the American Medical Association* reported that 'The controversy over pep pills is not confined to the United States. It is keeping doctors and athletes talking in Japan, Germany, Mexico, Sweden and other nations.' In England, it noted, Bannister's most prominent colleague on the sports medicine lecture circuit, Sir Adolphe Abrahams, was suggesting that the use of amphetamine might well be a legitimate technique for boosting athletic performance. [21] Yet despite all this activity, Bannister would claim that, prior to June 1957, the whole subject of drugs and runners had escaped his attention.

The subject of athletic doping had in fact come to public attention as early as 1953 when Abrahams published a letter on this topic in *The Times*. In 1952, he and Sir Arthur Porritt had founded the British Association of Medicine and Sport, headquartered at the British Olympic Association. [22] On 10 July 1953, Abrahams published a letter in *The Times* to announce that the new sports medicine group had recently discussed 'the principle of so-called "doping" of athletes, about which there is no little misconception and unnecessary perturbation'. The writer informed the readership of Britain's newspaper of record that 'official athletic bodies' had already expressed 'the opinion that the use of drugs to improve athletic performances should be forbidden'. [23] Over the course of the next two weeks, *The Times* published four letters commenting on Abrahams's report. The first of these letters noted that Abrahams had 'brought out into the open the discussions that have been going on in this and other countries about the doping of competitors in exhausting trials', thereby confirming that the issue of doping was being widely discussed, if not widely reported, at this time. The writer went on to say that in 1936 he had carried out 'an experiment on myself' that involved taking 20 and then 30 milligrams of amphetamine 'to improve my endurance in climbing'. [24] The second correspondent recalled an experiment performed in 1908 at Oxford in which a doctor administered oxygen to a rowing crew that went on to trounce its opponents in another boat. [25] The third letter reported that some rowers in the 1860s had used champagne as a training aid. [26] The fourth writer gave a realistic account of cyclists on the Continent using strychnine, caffeine and Benzedrine and suggested that 'the fashion for taking such stimulants seems to come and go, and at this moment there is very little of it indeed'. Anticipating the controversy of 1957, he considered and then dismissed the potential value of stimulants for the elite athlete:

> One cannot imagine a Reg Harris or Roger Bannister being able to maintain their superb degree of fitness on such a routine, and of course it is a fact that they could not do it. . . . One might envisage the four-minute mile being attempted by such a doped athlete, but in order to make such an attempt he would have to do the necessary training to make himself supremely fit. If he them took dope the side effects of that dope would almost certainly be disastrous, and he would be much more likely to do his worst time ever rather than a best time. [27]

In April 1955, Abrahams, now an honorary medical adviser to the International Athletic Board, reported 'a persistent belief among athletes that there must be something [drugs or medicine] that would create energy or postpone fatigue'. [28] There is, then, reason to ask how Roger Bannister, a medical student and laboratory physiologist then approaching the climax of his career as an elite runner, could have remained unaware of this discussion until a rude awakening in June of 1957.

It is safe to say that Bannister could not possibly have remained unaware of Abrahams, whose brother Harold had won the Olympic gold medal in the 100-metre dash at the 1924 Paris Olympic Games – a story that has been immortalized in the film *Chariots of Fire* (1981). In the early 1950s Harold was covering Britain's elite running corps for *The Times*, and this of course included writing about Roger Bannister among others. [29] More importantly, Adolphe became from 1953 on Britain's most prominent commentator on the issue of doping athletes. Indeed, the 1953 letter to *The Times* initiated a series of published commentaries which are especially notable for Abrahams's consistent refusal to adopt a moralistic position on athletes' use of drugs.

The first commentary of 1953 makes a number of points that remain essential to any thoughtful analysis of the doping problem. First, it turns out that the 'official athletic bodies' that had forbidden the use of drugs had also requested a definition of what 'a drug' actually was. The British Association of Sport and Medicine had been unable to come up with a satisfactory definition, 'since a comprehensive prohibition was clearly ridiculous'. The stimulants that concerned Abrahams as a physician were 'those drugs which by inhibiting or paralysing the protective mechanisms that normally guard against over-exhaustion could contribute to a greater physical output'. He was not the first to argue that such drugs were potentially dangerous to those who took them, and he was confident that 'no reputable practitioner in this country' would encourage their use. At this point, however, Abrahams reverses field and asks his readers to consider, 'for the sake of argument', a scenario featuring a drug 'capable of conferring enhanced athletic efficiency' that posed no medical hazard whatsoever and that was 'universally available' – thereby eliminating the problem of limited access for a favoured few. 'What objection could be raised against its use?' he asks. 'Only that – to use the question-begging term – it would be unsporting to enable athletes to surpass records achieved by the giants of the past, who lacked that advantage. I do not think the conscience of the sporting world would or need be disturbed,' he concludes. Here is the first occasion on which Abrahams opens the door to the legitimate use of performance-enhancing drugs by athletes. Two years later, in his lecture of April 1955, he emphasized the uselessness of drugs in sport and the power of the placebo effect. And once again he condemned any 'drugs that could stimulate the body to exertion beyond its normal limits of fatigue'. [30]

On 16 June 1957, Abrahams made his own contribution to the public discussion that had been ignited by Dr Berger's claims about amphetamine use by athletes. 'Should athletes take "pep" drugs?' appeared in the *Sunday Times* and reiterated his basic themes, including the warning against narcotics that 'remove the inhibitions that ensure self-preservation' and the idea that any power that drugs possessed was due to the power of suggestion. Here, too, he argued that distinguishing between the legitimate and illegitimate medication of athletes was anything but a straightforward exercise. It is not easy, he says,

> to draw the line where legitimate stimulation ends and reprehensible 'doping' begins; the distinction is largely a matter of opinion and conscience. Was it, for example, 'unsporting' to use oxygen in ascending Everest? . . . Are we to refrain from 'drugs' that sharpen the appetite, improve the digestion and so contribute to physical well-being?

The widespread contention that 'drugs' were 'unsporting' presented the thoughtful observer with what he called 'a debatable situation'. [31] Such open scepticism towards the ethic of sportsmanship must have disturbed many of his readers. [32] He invoked the oxygen scenario a year later in a lecture to the Society for the Study of Addiction: 'If it were practicable to construct a tunnel with oxygen-enriched atmosphere in which runners competed, record performances would be accomplished. But would this be approved? If amphetamine and cortisone can directly release another reserve of energy, are they not to be accepted as contributing to normal physiological well-being?' [33] Once again, Abrahams had chosen to open the Pandora's box that lurks in any honest discussion of human enhancements – the problem of defining 'normal' human functioning at any particular time and place. On 23 June 1960, Abrahams told his audience at the annual meeting of the British Medical Association that, although he expected only fractional improvements in world records, 'It was possible that biochemists might find some drug which would enhance the speed and force of muscular contraction, leading to new records'. He was followed at the podium by Dr Roger Bannister, who spoke about 'Some physiological factors limiting athletic performance', with special emphasis on oxygen transport to the muscles. [34] We are left to wonder whether this was the first occasion on which Bannister had heard Abrahams talk about performance-enhancing drugs.

As far as I have been able to determine, the only doping scenario Bannister discussed in public before the controversy of June 1957 was the possibility of supplying pure oxygen to the athlete. 'It seems clear,' he wrote in his 1955 memoir,

> that if an athlete could find a practicable way of breathing high concentrations of oxygen, no middle distance records would be beyond his grasp. Whether such help is justifiable in what is after all only a sport belongs to ethics rather than physiology. It is my personal opinion that it is not justifiable. [35]

He made the same point in his remarks to the Harveian Society of London on 13 April 1955: 'Whether it was practicable to breathe oxygen in high concentrations while running a race it was difficult to say. If it were, no middle-distance records would be beyond the runner's grasp, but whether this was desirable in what was after all only a sport was highly questionable.' 'In conclusion, Dr Bannister said that the various physiological studies were undoubtedly a help to athletics, but the main thing was the athlete's enjoyment of his performance irrespective of the standard.' [36]

Roger Bannister's measured remarks on the ethics of performance enhancement point to the core of the doping issue, which is the principle of self-restraint. Contemplating the swollen physique of a female Russian shot-putter in 1957, his feeling was that 'the price of victory is far too big'. [37] In the Soviet Union, ambition had trumped moderation and produced excess in pursuit of a performance that was simply not worth so great a departure from the human norm he accepted without protest. 'An absolute physical barrier does exist,' he wrote the same year, 'but where is a matter of speculation. Everyone agrees that a three-minute mile is impossible unless a new human being is bred, more greyhound than man, and it is axiomatic that to a process which cannot continue indefinitely, like record-breaking, there must be a limit.' [38] A significant point here is that Bannister was evidently untroubled by the certainty that human beings would eventually encounter this limit, since the alternative to this untroubled state of mind is what we call the doping mentality. [39]

The evidence presented up to this point helps us to understand the cultural status of chemical performance enhancement in British sport half a century ago. Most importantly, the conflict between sportsmanship and athletic ambition that had been intensifying since the beginning of the century now had a pharmacological dimension that could not be ignored.

As the first respondent to Abrahams put it in 1953, society was now confronting the question of 'where would sporting competition end' in a world of drug-enhanced athletics. 'Either sporting competitions would be between bio-chemists of the future, or they would go down by involving all competitors in a problem of personal honour versus chemical enterprise.' [40] The difference between Bannister's philosophy and that of Abrahams amounted to just such a conflict between 'personal honour' and an openness to the fruits of 'chemical enterprise'. At the same time, we must keep in mind that this discussion was occurring at an early phase of the modern doping debate. British sports officials were intent on banning 'drugs' whose objectionable nature they could not even define. Britain's most prominent sports physician (Abrahams) was telling his audiences that 'doping' was 'largely a matter of opinion and of conscience'. [41] His own objections to drugs were that they were ineffective and potentially dangerous, not that they constituted an offence against the amateur ethos – at this time no one knew whether drugs could really stimulate athletes. [42] Indeed, Abrahams's evident interest in the oxygen priming of athletes was a clear challenge to the amateur ethic of self-restraint. Even Roger Bannister, who has remained an icon of drug-free sport during the age of steroids, did not address the doping issue until Dr Berger forced him to do so.

Amphetamine drugs were common in Britain and the United States during the 1950s. [43] All the major powers of the Second World War had given 'pep pills' to their soldiers and pilots, and this contributed to their widespread use beyond their clinical application to cases of narcolepsy and depression. [44] In Japan the military stocks of the drug quickly found their way into the civilian sector after the surrender of 1945. This meant that 'amphetamine was available to anyone in Japan, and it was taken by students who wanted to be more effective in study or in sports, by night workers, and by some people for curiosity or because they wanted to enjoy night life'. [45] Amphetamine was also becoming a lifestyle drug in Britain. 'The drug is being increasingly prescribed,' the *British Medical Journal* reported in 1950,

> for its stimulant psychological effect, and its employment for this purpose is more questionable. It is being taken to renew the flagging energies of chronic over-workers, to keep playboys and playgirls awake when they should be asleep, to give an evanescent sense of well-being to apathetic, melancholic and frustrated people, and to relieve the depression of 'the morning after' in alcoholic subjects. [46]

Another recreational amphetamine subculture could be found a decade later among the British residents of West Africa, where one visitor was 'startled to see a tin of "dexedrine" (dexamphetamine) being handed around at midnight to facilitate continuation of their revels. This was regarded as a normal practice in a community tending to go in for marathon social activities at the week-end.' [47]

'Benzedrine' (amphetamine sulphate) tablets were introduced in the United States in 1932 as 'the first volatile nasal vasoconstrictor' for swollen nasal tissues. [48] They entered British medicine in 1936 'to diminish fatigue and worry' and to serve a number of other clinical purposes. [49] By 1953 there were five popular brands of 'pocket inhalers' containing amphetamine on sale in Britain. [50] At a time when the therapeutic dose for narcolepsy was 10 or 20 milligrams, the 'benzedrine' inhaler contained 325 milligrams of amphetamine to treat the common cold. While amphetamines fell under schedules 1 and 7 of the Poisons Rule, inhaled amphetamine was exempted from restriction. [51] (Sex hormones such as testosterone were also unregulated in Britain at this time.) [52] In other words, any adult in Britain could easily get hold of as much amphetamine as he or she might want. As late as 1962 one physician wrote to the *British Medical Journal*: 'The drug should not be available for self-administration in this casual fashion. The regulations should, at the very least, make it impossible to buy these inhalers without a prescription.' [53]

Associating drugs with athletic performance was common in advertisements during the 1950s in both lay and medical publications. Drug promotions in medical journals frequently used images of athletes to promote the sale of stimulants and other drugs. A golfer and a lacrosse player appear in a 1953 ad for 'Dexedrine' (amphetamine) tablets. [54] Squads of lifeguards dramatize the benefits of the '98% pure medicinal glucose' called Glucodin. [55] Teams of rowers appear in an ad for a penicillin preparation. [56] A cricket player takes a mighty swing in an ad for Hypon Tablets, an analgesic. [57] A heavily muscled pole-vaulter soars over the bar for Achromycin V, a broad-spectrum antibiotic therapy. [58] The glucose drink 'Lucozade' was advertised in 1953 in a London tabloid as an 'essential food for the athlete' and as 'a wonderful stimulant' for manual labourers such as miners. [59] In 1959 a governmental food standards committee proposed the regulation of glucose drinks at a time when inhaled amphetamine was still unregulated. We should note that half a century ago it did not occur to this committee to address the issue of performance enhancement. Its argument was rather that 'glucose beverages' should bear accurate labels, since 'they are held to have no special virtue from the medicinal point of view'. [60]

This is the pharmacological landscape in which the four-minute mile was finally achieved. As the Australian swimming coach Forbes Carlisle told me almost 50 years later: 'This was a different, and in most parts of the world, an innocent era in which anti-doping laws had not been thought of.' It simply did not occur to him that performance aids might be unethical. [61] 'Each race is an experiment,' Roger Bannister wrote in 1955. [62] To the best of my knowledge, he has never commented on whether he considered experimenting with drugs at a time when he was both an experimental physiologist and a physician in training who was bent on taking the mile record where no one had taken it before. It is hard to imagine that he did not at some point think about amphetamine what *The Lancet* had thought in 1936, that it would 'be very interesting in due course to learn exactly what it is capable of doing within the limits of safety'. [63]

Roger Bannister's alleged connection to the age of steroids is Franz Stampfl, a track and field coach who was born in Vienna in 1913 and arrived in England in the mid-1930s. Stampfl was the coach of Bannister's friend and fellow miler Chris Brasher, and Bannister valued his advice. [64] In 1955 Stampfl moved to Australia to coach at Melbourne University. Stampfl regarded himself as a 'scientific' coach. 'I introduced biological and physiological approaches to running and mechanics to throwing,' he told an interviewer before his death in 1995. [65] In the late 1970s he was coaching the Australians Bev Francis and Gael Mulhall in throwing events. Eventually, both of these women became power-lifting champions. Bev Francis turned to bodybuilding and became the most heavily muscled woman in the world. In 1987 Gael Mulhall Martin, who had competed in the shot and discus at the 1980 and 1984 Olympic Games, told a federal panel that she had used steroids throughout her career as a thrower. (She had tested positive for steroid use at the 1981 Pan Pacific Conference Games.) Given the nature of the athlete-coach relationship, it is quite possible that Stampfl was either tolerating or encouraging her use of performance-enhancing drugs. At this time she, another female athlete and head coach Kelvin Giles accused the Australian Institute of Sport of supplying banned drugs to athletes. [66] In a book published in 2000, the Australian discus thrower Werner Reiterer says that Stampfl's advice to Martin was: 'Take heaps of flak and deny it.' He also recalls a scene from about 1980 between another boy and Stampfl. Their exchange of words suggested this young athlete expected the coach to give him steroids, at which point an enraged Stampfl is said to have told his young charge to keep his mouth shut. [67]

Roger Bannister's association with Franz Stampfl is one more reminder that the potent combination of scientific training and ambition existed before the steroid epidemic that accelerated during the 1960s, and that the history of modern doping has been a continuous development rather than an abrupt fall into hormone doping. Indeed, the commentaries of Bannister's lecture circuit companion, the physician Adolphe Abrahams, make it clear that whether one chose to explore or condemn athletic doping was still 'a matter of opinion and of conscience' half a century ago. By way of conclusion, we might note that a significant number of sports physicians would eventually adopt a similar attitude towards hormone doping during the age of steroids that followed the amphetamine era. [68]

## Notes

[1] 'AMA to study drugs in sports; Use in four-minute mile hinted', *New York Times*, 6 June 1957.

[2] 'Athletes deny use of drugs', *The Times* (London), 7 June 1957.

[3] 'Drug-use charge denied by milers', *New York Times*, 7 June 1957.

[4] 'Athletes deny use of drugs'.

[5] 'The milers speak up', *Newsweek*, 17 June 1957, p. 100.

[6] 'Drug-use charge denied by milers'.

[7] 'The milers speak up'.

[8] 'AMA to study drugs in sports'.

[9] Ibid.

[10] 'Coaches condemn drug-use charges', *New York Times*, 16 June 1957.

[11] 'Athletes deny use of drugs'.

[12] Adolphe Abrahams, 'Should athletes take "pep" drugs?' *Sunday Times* (London), 16 June 1957.

[13] 'Resolution on use of stimulants, such as amphetamine, in sports', *Journal of the American Medical Association* [hereafter *JAMA*], 164 (13 July 1957), p. 1244.

[14] Review of E.W. Adams, *Drug addiction* (1937), *The Lancet*, 11 Sept. 1937, p. 634.

[15] 'So specialized have officials in sport become that they are inclined to fail to appreciate what goes on in other sports than their own particular one. However, I think such people have quite a lot to learn, at least in the form of being forewarned, from a practice that has occurred for many years in the sport of cycling. Three years ago I did a thorough investigation of this subject of doping among cyclists on the Continent, and I found the habit quite common. The three principal drugs that were used were strychnine, caffeine and benzedrine.' C.R. Woodard, '"Doping" of Athletes' [letter], *The Times*, 23 July 1953.

[16] 'Athletes report use of "pep pills"', *New York Times*, 8 June 1957; 'The milers speak up'.

[17] Roger Bannister, *The first four minutes* (London, 1955), pp. 109, 110. 'Breathing and circulatory measurements could be made while I ran, I used the motor-driven treadmill in the laboratory on which the speed and gradient could be altered so as to exhaust the toughest athlete in a few minutes. In time I learnt to repeat my performance on the treadmill so that I could study the effect on my performance of changes in body temperature, in the acidity of the blood, and in the composition of the air breathed in.' See *The first four minutes*, p. 119.

[18] 'Physiology of athletic training', *British Medical Journal* [hereafter *BMJ*], 19 Sept. 1953, p. 670.

[19] 'Medical aspects of athletics', *BMJ*, 23 April 1955, p. 1026.

[20] Roger Bannister, 'Amateurism in sport . . . is it really necessary', *Sunday Times* (London), 2 June 1957; Roger Bannister, 'Ibbotson can run a 3min. 55sec. mile', *Sunday Times*, 21 July 1957; Roger Bannister, 'Big set-back for Russian athletes', *Sunday Times*, 25 Aug. 1957.

[21] 'Amphetamines, athletes, and performance', *JAMA*, 168 (11 Oct. 1958), p. 775.

[22] Adolphe Abrahams and Arthur Porritt, 'Sport and medicine' [letter], *The Lancet*, 12 July 1952, p. 90. Porritt, a New Zealander, had finished third at the 1924 Paris Olympic Games behind Abrahams's brother Harold in the 100-metre dash. He eventually served as Governor-General of New Zealand.

[23] Adolphe Abrahams, '"Doping" of athletes' [letter], *The Times*, 10 July 1953.

[24] H. Crichton-Miller, '"Doping" of athletes', *The Times*, 14 July 1953.

[25] J.D. Casswell, '"Doping" of athletes', *The Times*, 15 July 1953.

[26] O.D.H. Clauson, '"Doping" of athletes', *The Times*, 18 July 1953.

[27] C.R. Woodard, '"Doping" of athletes', *The Times*, 23 July 1953.

[28] This is a paraphrase of Abrahams's actual remarks. See 'Athletic training', *JAMA*, 157 (16 April 1955), p. 1430.

[29] See, for example, 'Bannister runs a good mile', *The Times*, 8 June 1952.

[30] This is a paraphrase of Abrahams's actual remarks. See 'Athletic training', *JAMA*, 157.

[31] Abrahams, 'Should athletes take "pep" drugs?'.

[32] This statement certainly disturbed an editorialist at the *Journal of the American Medical Association*, who commented: 'His statement is open to attack on the ground of sportsmanship – particularly in amateur athletics. The statement also emphasizes the use, rather than the abuse, of amphetamine. Yet is even judicious use safe? And if it is, what are the perils of misuse?' 'Amphetamines, athletes, and performance', *JAMA*, 168.

[33] Quoted in ibid. Abrahams was not the first British physician to wonder about the possible effects of these drugs on athletic performance. See 'Cortisone and athletic performance' [letter], *BMJ*, 13 Dec. 1952, p. 1320.

[34] This is a paraphrase of Abrahams's actual remarks. See 'The contribution of medicine to efficiency in sport', *BMJ*, 9 July 1960, p. 130.

[35] Bannister, *The first four minutes*, p. 119. Bannister made the same point in his lecture to the Harveian Society of London on 13 April 1955: 'Whether it was practicable to breathe oxygen in high concentrations while running a race it was difficult to say. If it were, no middle-distance records would be beyond the runner's grasp, but whether this was desirable in what was after all only a sport was highly questionable.' This is a paraphrase of Bannister's actual remarks. See 'Medical aspects of athletics'.

[36] This is a paraphrase of Bannister's actual remarks. See 'Medical aspects of athletics'.

[37] Bannister, 'Big set-back for Russian athletes'.

[38] Bannister, 'Ibbotson can run a 3min. 55sec. mile'.

[39] Bannister was also a canny critic of the amateurism of his day. 'The social stigma of professionalism is now almost dead,' he wrote in 1957, and he rejected the idea that the motivations of professional athletes were necessarily unwholesome. What mattered most to him was the 'spirit' of the game. 'It is the leaven of amateurism,' he wrote, 'that gives British professional sport an integrity that is lacking in many other countries.' In the last analysis, however, his deepest loyalty was to the amateur ethos: 'Whatever the incidental reward an amateur athlete may receive, I cannot help feeling that if a fat purse had been handed to Chataway when he defeated Kuts, the plaudits of the crowd would have been dulled and the glory of the victory in some way tarnished.' See Roger Bannister, 'Amateurism in sport . . . is it really necessary?' *Sunday Times*, 2 June 1957.

[40] Crichton-Miller, '"Doping" of athletes'.

[41] Abrahams, 'Should athletes take "pep" drugs?'

[42] Responding to the 1957 controversy, Prof. Thomas K. Cureton of the University of Illinois commented: 'The major point is the release of potential energy. Obviously a quick release makes for a better effort. At this time, no scientist knows whether drugs can create this release or whether an athlete who takes them is merely wasting his time.' See 'The milers speak up'. Published research on the performance-enhancing effects of amphetamine on athletes first appeared in 1959. See Gene M. Smith and Henry K. Beecher, 'Amphetamine sulfate and athletic performance', *JAMA*, 170 (30 May 1959), pp. 542–57.

[43] 'Dr [Herbert] Berger estimated that next to aspirins, amphetamines are the most commonly used compounds in the nation. Drug manufacturers produce 6,000,000,000 amphetamine pills each year, he estimated. This is thirty-five pills for each man, woman and child in the United States.' See 'AMA to study drugs in sports'.

[44] See, for example, 'Energy in pills', *Business Week*, 15 Jan. 1944, pp. 40, 42, 44; Maj. Gen. David N.W. Grant, '"Pep" Pills for bomber pilots', *Science Digest*, 15 (June 1944), pp. 85–7.

[45] 'Abuse of amphetamine', *The Lancet*, 22 Sept. 1956, p. 632.

[46] 'Psychological effects of amphetamine', *BMJ*, 25 Feb. 1950, p. 476.

[47] 'Amphetamine in the tropics', *BMJ*, 26 Nov. 1960, p. 1601.

[48] T.C. Black, 'Amphetamine' [letter], *BMJ*, 11 July 1953, p. 96.

[49] 'New preparations', *The Lancet*, 8 Aug. 1936, p. 354.

[50] *BMJ*, 13 March 1954, p. 616.

[51] 'Amphetamine addiction', *BMJ*, 10 July 1954, p. 101.

[52] 'Sale of hormones', *The Lancet*, 23 April 1955, p. 875.

[53] See 'Amphetamine inhalers', *BMJ*, 8 Sept. 1962, p. 674.

[54] *The Lancet*, 28 Nov. 1953, p. iii.

[55] *The Lancet*, 13 March 1954, p. 27.

[56] *The Lancet*, 3 April 1954, p. 9.

[57] *The Lancet*, 5 Jan. 1952, p. 11.

[58] *BMJ*, 4 Oct. 1958, p. 23.

[59] *Daily Herald* (London), 31 July 1953.
[60] 'Regulation of soft drinks', *BMJ*, 7 March 1959, p. 637.
[61] Personal communication from Forbes Carlisle, 3 Dec. 2000.
[62] Bannister, *The first four minutes*, p. 121
[63] 'Benzedrine', *The Lancet*, 19 Dec. 1936, p. 1476.
[64] Bannister, *The first four minutes*, p. 186.
[65] 'The sports factor with Amanda Smith', Radio National Australia, 28 July 2000.
[66] See http://wso.williams.edu/listserv/tfselect/Sep1598-Oct198/msg00121.html and http://www.olympics.smh.com.au/athletics/2000/08/29/FFXGMJVOFCC.html, accessed 29 March 2002; also http://www.newcastle.edu.au/discipline/history/superscripts/2001/matas.html, accessed 30 March 2002. See also 'Athlete's urine sample poured down sink', *Sydney Morning Herald*, 15 June 1989; 'No medal for truth', *Sydney Morning Herald*, 14 Jan. 1989; 'Coach's drug denial', *Sydney Morning Herald*, 14 Dec. 1988; 'AIS head knew of drug use: Martin', *Sydney Morning Herald*, 8 Dec. 1988.
[67] Werner Reiterer, *Positive* (Sydney, 2000), p. 24.
[68] See John Hoberman, 'Sports physicians and the doping crisis in elite sport', *Clinical Journal of Sport Medicine*, 12 (2002), pp. 203–8.

# Training Theory and Why Roger Bannister was the First Four-Minute Miler

Arnd Krüger

> Ladies and Gentlemen, here is the result of event number nine, the One Mile: First number 41, R.G. Bannister formerly of Exeter and Merton Colleges, with a time which is a new meeting and track record and which subject to ratification will be a new English Native, British National, British All Comers', European, British Empire and World's Record. The time is three [and the following words were lost in a roar] minutes 59 point four seconds. [1]

## Introduction

In competing for the public's interest each sport plays a different role. Track and field athletics have been of major interest in most of the world and are today – together with football – the sport practised in most countries. In athletics, track events generally draw more attention than the field events. In the Anglo-Saxon world the mile has been hyped for many years, more so than most other events. The reasons for this, I suggest, is that is the mile requires a delicate mixture of alactic and lactic anaerobic as well as aerobic metabolisms and it is slower than the half-mile and thus presents the opportunity for more tactical possibilities. Since the 1930s the four minute barrier – the 'Miracle Mile' [2] – was much talked and written about.

For the middle-distance runner, the right mixture of training elements is difficult to determine. For Hoole, in his late-nineteenth-century book on *The Science and Art of Training*, [3] there was still the unity of art and science, as for him science was nothing but a series of rules to be followed by athletes. Coaching science does not believe in 'art' or in miracles. On the whole, there ought to be a good explanation why certain things happen in sports and they have to be duplicable to make them scientific. 'General training theory' only started to develop in the 1950s and many of the parameters used today to objectify reasons for success make predictions about future accomplishments, and organize training in such a way as to increase the likelihood of success, were not measured nor observed in the 1950s. [4]

However, Roger Bannister was a keen scientist and described many of his subjective observations and feelings in his training and races from which one can draw conclusions if these have been properly recorded and read. [5] Franz Stampfl, who advised Brasher, Chataway and Bannister, has also written about Bannister's training. The Austrian Stampfl was one of the better coaches at the time. He could mix the Freiburg style of scientific interval training with the training approaches of the Anglo-Saxon world. [6] His awareness of two different paradigms allowed him to be more responsive to different parameters of the effect that training had on his athletes. I am not suggesting that scientifically-based training is better, but it relies more on the measurement of internal data (starting with such simple things as heart rate) and thus tries to objectify the effort involved in training. [7] Rudolf Harbig (who died in action in 1944 on the Eastern Front, but in 1954 still held the fantastic 800 metres world record), Joseph Barthel (Olympic 1500 metres champion in 1952) and the legendary Gordon Pirie were all coached by Woldemar Gerschler, the head of the Freiburg University physical education department, and medically advised by Herbert Reindell, later to become one of the most famous professors of sports medicine worldwide.

As John Bale has remarked, these runners were all coached by scientists, 'but Bannister was a scientist'. [8] If you do not have objective data, you have to translate the subjective. As Bannister was basically self-coached and only advised by Stampfl, who did not watch much of his training, he had to develop a very astute sense of observation, using his scientific training to organize his training and communication with his adviser. I am not a native speaker of English but I have been around the international scene in middle-distance running for a long time as athlete and coach, so I venture to translate the training of the time into the terms of present-day general training theory. [9]

In trying to answer the question why Bannister was the first to break the four-minute barrier, my basic argument is that while he might certainly have trained more frequently, added proper altitude training and picked a faster track (or had the existing one made faster), other than that he did little that was wrong. I will shortly review his major competitors to show in which ways they were not as complete an athlete as Bannister. In respect to the British duodecimal system of the time, I will give 12 reasons to explain Roger Bannister's strengths.

## Twelve good reasons

### *Respect for the Oxbridge tradition and British sports*

There are many different traditions of running longer distances. The Anglo-American tradition cherished the mile much more than many other distance. Thus the mile was more important for Bannister than for a mainland European. A tradition is like a paradigm as it emphasizes certain aspects of training over others. According to Karl Popper, any theory ought to be testable. For Popper the sciences existed as a whole. He rejected the divisions between the different sciences and pointed out that there were just problems to be solved and that the differentiation between the sciences is arbitrary. This is also the basis for 'coaching theory' as coaches do not care too much why somebody is running faster – as long as he or she *is* running faster. Athletics makes testing easy because the outcome is on the track: if you are winning or setting a new record, the chances are that your theory was better than the theory your opponent was using – all other things being equal. Testing a present paradigm functions best when you are aware of previous tests of either the same paradigm or the basis of the current one. [10]

Knowing and respecting the training of those before you gives you the advantage that you learn a lot about their testing of a training paradigm and thus you can learn from their trials and errors. Throughout Bannister's writings there is a great respect for the Oxbridge tradition. In fact, he tried as far as possible to copy much of this tradition for his own life. To copy fine athletes such as Jack Lovelock or his non-Oxbridge hero Sydney Wooderson does not help to surpass them, [11] but it is a good basis for at least equalling their performances. Bannister tried to merge into their thinking and added his own Oxford breed of rationality. [12]

## *Methodology of the art and science of training*

To classify Bannister's training one has to look at the development of training in middle and long distances. For this there are several possible approaches: One can look at the emphasis of science textbooks and journals on endurance training and middle- and long-distance running. One can look at the training books written by top athletes and their coaches, at their biographies or autobiographies, or general histories of athletics. [13] It should not be overlooked that the training of internationally-renowned athletes has a considerable influence – for better or worse – on the art and science of training. Journals such as *Track Coach* (formerly *Track Technique*), *Track & Field Coaches Review* or *Modern Athlete and Coach, Leichtathletik, Leichtathletiktraining* or the *Amicale des Entraîneurs d'Athlétisme* have always devoted some pages to the training of famous athletes, trying to discover their success. To some extent it might even be possible to use the method of oral history, at least for some of the period. [14] One could, of course, also look the progress in particular events – in our case the mile. [15]

There is a trend in the history of any science to assume that there is a constant improvement in the amount and quality of scientific knowledge available. Although this is partially true, one should not forget that knowledge is not only gained but also lost over time. What does not coincide with the dominating paradigm, what is published in the 'wrong' places, is often disregarded.

In the current context I will use all of the sources available and will try to put them into Kuhn's methodological framework [16] and the work of others who have studied the history of science. I will, therefore, look at the major paradigmatic changes, the turning points of the development, and not so much at the fine differentiation in what Kuhn called 'puzzle solving'. According to the dominating training paradigm, we can differentiate between four distinct dominating theories with which the major concern in the training rules and habits can be explained in the last 150 years. What follows is a discussion of these forms: natural training; psychologically or learning-oriented training; physiologically-oriented training; and individualized training.

It is very unlikely that at any given time there is but one paradigm. After all, even today much of the running success of the athletes from Kenya is attributed to their natural way of training in their youth more than to any scientific approach [17] and Native Americans have always been of interest and influenced the thinking of modern scientifically trained athletes. [18] But it should not be overlooked that such an overlapping of paradigms is commensurable with Kuhn's theory; that any new paradigm only assumes that it can explain the observed facts better than any previous theory. So, by a modern definition, the Kenyans do not run better because of natural training but because their coronary system is superior, as they have laid a broad physiological base by long-distance hiking and jogging from a very early age in high altitude, thus improving tremendously their oxygen-carrying capacity through an increase in haemoglobin and myoglobin. [19]

The Frenchman Georges Hébert (1875–1957) was arguably the best theoretician of the *natural* method. [20] Although his main emphasis was the education of youth, he took charge of the Collège d'Athlètes in Reims, where the French tried to prepare their athletes for the Olympic Games of 1916. [21] His principal purpose was a well versed physical preparation programme. [22] His training included, therefore, many less specific elements that were to assure a sound athletic basis. The showdown between the natural method and more specific learning-oriented methods came at the 1912 Olympics. These were the first Olympic Games to contain all the distance races. In the heats of the 5,000 metres Jean Bouin of France, disciple of Hébert, had set a world record in 15 minutes 5 seconds. In the finals he was beaten by the young but later legendary Hannes Kolehmainen of Finland in a fantastic new world record of 14 minutes 36.6 seconds, beating Bouin by one-tenth of a second. As Kolehmainen took part in six races over nine days at the Olympic Games, winning them all and covering 41 kilometres in doing so, he can be considered one of the all-time Olympic greats. His success over Bouin seemed to prove that 'scientific' (and that meant at first 'specific') training was better than an all-round preparation. It also seemed to show that the *Turner* and *gymnastic* notion – that you had to have an all-round training on top of which you could specialize – was not valid in the distance races. Hébert only stands for a certain direction of a wide field of what can be called a 'natural training'.

Kolehmainen came from a family of distance runners. His older brothers were part of the American professional circuit. They advised him on what to do. By the standards of the day it was quite a lot of running (twice a day): He learned a certain style, certain race paces, and to behaved like a successful athlete. [23]

## *The learning-oriented approach*

It is difficult to differentiate between natural and learning-oriented training. A close examination of the writing of Alfred Shrubb illuminates elements of the learning-oriented approach since he was practising race speed and tried to stretch out the distance he was capable of at a relatively steady pace. His biography even claimed that he 'must be the most scientific and at the same time the most scientifically-trained runner who has ever taken to either the track or cross-country' [24]

The developing discipline of sport psychology (1913 – the first international conference, [25] first behaviourist publications by J.B. Watson) provided the scientific basis for the learning experience. The learning-oriented approach resembles mostly a certain brand of behaviourism. Behaviour was typically considered a response to a stimulus. What became accepted practice in experimental psychology, particularly in the United States and Scandinavia, also influenced the theory of training. Kolehmainen represented the beginning of the era of the 'Flying Finns' and those who followed their theories. Although learning was often not mentioned in the theoretical background, it is typical of the methods of Paavo Nurmi, Ville Ritola, Edwin Wide and others that they tried to learn a certain track behaviour. [26] The emphasis was on style and on steady pace. The symbol for this period was Nurmi's stopwatch, which was to assure even pace and the control of it even during the race.

In the training books of the time there are lengthy discussions about 'proper' style. But style is not discussed in terms of 'running economy' nor 'energy expenditure'. [27] Instead it is considered in terms of learning and movement behaviour. Self-observation and other forms of bio-feedback are, therefore, important to learn for the proper style in a stimulus-response fashion. [28] The capability for sudden bursts in a race was also considered as part of the learning process and not a matter of creatine phosphate availability and other processes of energy provision. [29]

I am not sure whether this emphasis on style and running behaviour does not have something to do with the similar thinking of the *Turners* and gymnasts. [30] Even when weight training was recommended, it was done to learn how to spurt in the way of champion athletes. [31] It can therefore also be considered part of a behaviouristic approach. This was a time when learning theory was dominated by behaviourism. Motor learning was supposed to take place when movements were repeated sufficiently often in the proper form. This was also the reason why training should not be all-out but should always be done in the proper style to assure that the racing style was learned.

The IOC conference in Lausanne in 1913 was the first attempt to link sport, movement behaviour and motor learning. With much deliberation and the formulation of results, it can be considered a 'consensus conference'. Natural, psychological and physiological training was discussed and it was concluded that each sport had its very specific requirements in all three respects. [32] De Coubertin's work reveals the shift: In 1916 he still insisted that in 'the training for distance running you need neither measure the distance nor take the time for your running with a stopwatch; all you need is a flat terrain sufficiently soft' – i.e. pure natural training. [33] After the First World War he stressed the role of psychology in contrast to physiology: 'There is another dangerous tendency to convert man physiologically into a thoroughbred without taking the psychological side and the will power into consideration, factors which are much more important.' [34] The muscular or 'kinaesthetic' sense became more and more significant and was at the centre of consideration.

### *The physiological approach*

The gruesome running style of Emil Zatopek can be considered to represent the victory of the physiological approach. It was no longer the style that could be learned and had to be maintained that counted, but the physiologically trained components of the athletic effort. The new approach had become dominant already before the war: Rudolf Harbig, who had broken the 800 metres world record by almost two seconds in 1939, had been the first top athlete who was trained by an exercise physiologist. [35] Reindell was the first physiologist who did reasonably accurate heart X-rays with a contrasting substance that permitted him to measure the size of the heart and thus measure the increase of the heart's size by training. While previously the athletic heart was considered dangerous, heart enlargement was now considered important for athletic success. [36] Theoretically, this is the birth of the rationale for interval training, which was the fastest way to enlarge the heart, though in practice Lauri Pihkala, the great Finnish coach, had already described it as 'terrace-training' in 1930. [37] Harbig's coach Woldemar Gerschler worked closely with Reindell. [38] Gerschler later become the coach of Gordon Pirie [39] and many other middle- and long-distance runners. An interval kind of training that stressed physiological elements became the norm and was later used by such great runners as Jim Ryun (trained by Bill Easton). [40]

In terms of international success the best performances during the war years obviously came from countries that were least involved in the Second World War. [41] The Swedish system had its best results then, with world-record holders such as Arne Andersson and Gunder Hägg. This was a *fartlek*-based training system, which tried to combine already established elements of the natural method (by training mainly in nature) with a physiological approach (a form of interval training to improve the cardiovascular system in an efficient way). [42] As in the case of Mihalyi Igloi [43] and Arthur Lydiard, [44] this was the first generation of coaches that personally had a global impact. Both had, however, one principle difference: While Igloi's runners trained with the main elements of physical conditioning side by side and were therefore in a reasonable race shape all year long, Lydiard's runners trained one element after another and were therefore more capable of achieving their optimal racing form for the most important race of the year. [45] It is also interesting to note that Igloi's training still contained many elements of the previous period in that he defined the different training pace not by a time that should be reached but by a certain running style that should be run (e.g. 'good swing tempo'). The significance of 'good form' is, however, stressed more by other coaches. [46] The importance of form and learning can also be seen by the most famous American coach, Bill Bowerman. He emphasized that his distance runners should have 'strength, pace judgement and speed, in that order'. [47] 'Pace judgement' is, of course, something very un-physiological, and can best be learned.

This is not to say that the relics of the previous system were not still there. Rather, the dominating paradigm had shifted in most countries. It can also be seen that there were many previous attempts to explain what was going on in training in physiological ways. John Hoberman assumes that the Physiological International had already considerable influence at the turn of the century. [48] While this is true for the scientific world, the athletic world did not really take notice of recent research results. Until the physiological revolution in the late 1930s, sports medicine was following the reality of training and was not going ahead. But even as late as 1979 David Costill could only conclude that the practice of training was still ahead of the theory. [49] In many fields today the practice is still much ahead of the theory. For a relatively brief period after the Second World War, the ideology of the Communist world started to have an impact on endurance training. [50] But in spite of all the scientific efforts, the success of the likes of Vladimir Kuts was soon over. In the middle distances a more natural approach like that of Percy Cerutty, the coach of Herb Elliot, [51] or that of the French with Michel Bernard was still visible, but the thinking had turned physiological even if many efforts were being made to strengthen natural instincts and will power. [52]

Modern society is characterized by individualization and globalization. [53] Bio-feedback processes to combine the motor learning side with the physiological side and other multifaceted forms of training are the order of the day. Training forms are no longer a secret but are repeated on a global scale. [54] Individualization dominates training regimes. Science is searching for the individual *reserves* that will improve individual performance. [55] Every training unit is recorded; the steering of training becomes very important. Lactate and other substances are measured during and after the training to make sure that the individual training is properly composed and has just the right doses. The assumption of Kenneth Doherty (1960) proved correct that

> in the not-distant future, coaches on the field will be supplemented by scientists in the laboratory. *Personal* reactions to the demand of activity on the field will be telemetered to the laboratory for immediate analysis and recommendation sent back to the coach on the field. The values of a training session will be measured by its effects on the person, rather than, as today, on a stop-watch. Even then, judgement will be a crucial element in good coaching, but it will be judged based on facts as well as on feelings and appearances. [56]

When we look at modern textbooks on endurance training it becomes obvious that a multifaceted approach is recommended by the best. [57]. There is still a dominance of physiological thinking. Psychological elements such as motivation are only used to explain variations in physiological data. The notion of physiological adaptation has superseded the idea of a motor learning and behaviourist approach in the middle and long distances.

For Bannister, who later developed into a prominent neurophysiologist, many of his training elements depend on the learning side of 'style'. Even the way this ought to be trained is purely behaviourist. [58] It is, however, questionable whether his training, which contained many elements of untimed running (=natural training) and time trials in race pace (=psychologically oriented training), can really be called purely *physiological* or whether it did not contain a lot of elements that made it very individual and very modern. [59]

According to Ericsson and his colleagues, it takes about ten years and/or 10,000 hours of deliberate practice to become an expert in anything, including sports. [60] This theory has been worked with for over ten years and seems to have its merit. In a recent overview, [61] it became obvious that, particularly in sports, the ten-year/10,000-hour rule seems to work. Looking at Bannister, it is often mentioned that he only started running the mile competitively after entering Oxford, i.e. eight years before the world record. It is frequently overlooked that he was a good runner at the age of 12 and did long-distance bicycle rides (up to 70 miles) in his youth. Thus his specific training at Oxford and later in London was on the basis of good genetic endowment and a considerable amount of early unspecific training. He therefore had done enough running and was in top form from the long-term point of view of sports expertise. [62]

### *Biomechanical efficiency*

Endurance running depends to a large extent on the biomechanical efficiency of the athlete. 'Style running' has tended to decline after the successes of Emil Zátopek, who seemed to have shown, as winner of the 5,000 metres in the Helsinki Olympics and 10,000 metres in the London and Helsinki Olympics, that the biomechanical is far less important than the physiological side of running. On the other hand, there is enough scientific evidence to show that 'efficiency' means 'economy', thus sparing energy, so important in the second half of the race. Photographs of Bannister while racing show that the vector of the rear leg leads very nicely and almost directly through the centre of gravity. It can also be seen that Bannister stretches his hind leg almost perfectly, thus making faultless use of the eccentric muscle contractions which are so energy-efficient. Of course, it is impossible to make an exact measurement of the running efficiency from photographs alone as there might be some muscular tightness that is difficult to observe, but Stampfl's call during the race to 'relax' and the fact that Bannister was able to follow his pace-setters into the back straight of the last lap all points to the probability of high efficiency in running. His own training advice also indicates that he was fully aware of the biomechanical efficiency. [63]

### *Strength training*

Bannister had a relatively good basis of mixing strength with endurance. At public school he had done some decent rowing, while at Oxford he did some hiking and mountain climbing. For Bale mountain climbing 'connotes freedom, a sensual engagement with nature and night-time, frolic, gambol, juissance, a visceral affection for wild places', [64] but this also has a training result. Climbing hills, just like jumping up hills in a Lydiard fashion ('hill springing'), improves strength endurance and also helps running efficiency through learning how to strike the centre of gravity even if one feels extremely exhausted and the legs have lost all their spring because of all the accumulated lactic acid. [65] Stampfl points out that 'sheer muscular strength is a fact of athletics which is too often overlooked by all but the throwing men'. [66] Together with his once-a-week 45-minute callisthenics session for most of the winter – as recommended by Stampfl – this gave Bannister a solid basis for strength endurance, so important for a solid acceleration at the end of a race. His own training advice mentions this, however, as 'speed' and says nothing about 'strength'.

### *Breaking the speed barrier = eccentric training*

The hiking and hill running has yet another important component. After all, it is not only uphill but also downhill. As Bannister describes it in his book, he went at super maximal speed downhill. Downhill running is most efficient to break the neuropsychological speed barrier and improve the eccentric capacity of the leg muscles. Of course, this has also a 'sensual engagement with nature', but most of all it is an efficient training means, a little more controlled, employed by the Olympic 800 metres and 1,500 metres champions Peter Snell and Pekka Vasala (the 1972 Olympic 1,500 metres champion) and by the Olympic 5,000 metres champions Murray Halberg (1960) and Lasse Viren (1972 and 1976), advised by Arthur Lydiard [67]

> I remember a race down from Snowdon Horseshoe with some friends. The wind sang in our ears and deafened us. Sometimes we tumbled, falling if we were lucky on a patch of grass, otherwise on hostile stones. We picked out likely landing places, as we jumped a ledge or boulder. Faster and faster we ran, each in turn leading until he slipped and was overtaken. Towards the bottom we could release ourselves from the agony of checking our descent that tore at the overworked muscles of our thighs. It was a glorious moment when the level ground brought us under control. [68]

This is a perfect description of breaking the speed barrier and doing eccentric work at the same time.

### *Interval training*

Bannister did not use the classical Freiburg (Gerschler/Reindell) type of interval training. The Freiburg style requires the recording of pulse values. The heart rate is brought up to 180 beats per minute and after a rest of jogging, when the pulse is back down to 120–130 beats per minute the athlete starts again. In Bannister's book there is no mention made anywhere about any heart-rate measurement as in many of the training books of the time, although such measurements were easy to make. Paavo Nurmi had used them already. The West German head coach Toni Nett wrote in 1954: 'The stop watch is your friend'; [69] and the East German Rolf Donath gave exact times for the interval before and after the pause in 1960. [70] Bannister's interval training of running, for example, 10 × 440 yards was to get used to race pace, to improve his stamina – not to get a strong heart. The stopwatch 'should be treated like a servant and the athlete should not allow himself to be dominated by it'. [71]. I find the scepticism towards science interesting for a medical doctor. Bannister reduced much to the question of mind over matter.

### *Anaerobic threshold training*

Bannister's early training was similar to that employed by runners in the first quarter of the twentieth century. He did one fast run over the distance to be covered in his next race. When he had already broken the world record, he recommended 'regular runs of two to four miles over the country during the inter-season period ... as with all training, it is better to cover a moderate distance three or four times a week than to take less frequent runs over longer distances'. [72] Similarly, Stampfl's weekly *fartlek* session from November until April over distances of five to ten miles is playing around the anaerobic threshold. [73] Many of these hard runs were on the anaerobic threshold if not slightly beyond. According to Harre, anaerobic threshold training increases the $VO^2$max which is a major component of aerobic capabilities. [74]

### *Test runs*

Bannister often used test runs or time trials mainly over three laps at race pace, improving the time month after month. These runs have the advantage of increasing the self-assurance that one can do the last quarter in the same pace as the test run. [75] As Bannister also did 10 × 440 yards at racing speed, he was certainly capable of good judgement of race pace, but interval training produces a Pavlov-type problem: Whenever tiredness is felt after a quarter of a mile, the body is rewarded by introducing a lap of jogging for two-and-a-half or three minutes. To put three quarter-miles at the same pace back to back at the same pace, the runner breaks up the interval Pavlov principle and becomes a good judge of race pace. [76]

### *Periodization*

The respect Bannister had for traditions, both of amateurism and the type of training that implied, meant that he followed the Oxbridge athletics schedule even upon graduation. The traditional Oxbridge season starts early, so there is a tradition of peaking early in the year. Bannister also had the advantage of trying to peak for the same date already one year before. [77]

The science of periodization was invented by Matveyer in the late 1950s by using the data of track and field, swimming and weight lifting of the previous years. Matveyer discovered that a cyclical form of training is superior to a non-cyclical one to peak when it counts. [78]

Bannister's training had a macro-cyclic structure, distinguishing between 'preliminary', 'early', 'middle', and 'peak'. It had a meso-cyclic structure in distinguishing between calendar months, and a micro-cyclic structure in distinguishing between weeks. [79] The main difference between the recommendations of Matveyer and Bannister lies in the latter recommending four equal weeks within the first three meso-cycles while Matveyer has each of the first three micro-cycles in each meso-cycle at a higher intensity than the previous one, while the fourth micro-cycle has a reduced intensity before starting again. Matveyer thus made use of the super-compensation theory, [80] which is not mentioned by Bannister. For the 1950s, Bannister is relatively modern in that he is fully aware of periodization and makes thorough use of it. He is even more modern than Matveyer was at the same time by using a final pre-race micro cycle of ten days, thus breaking up the one-week cycle. [81] By running the sub-four minute mile first, he showed that he peaked when it counted.

### *Programmes for several years*

'It was not the Oxford method to rush at things. You contemplate, you consider, and then on rare occasions you act.' [82] Bannister's respect for tradition makes a lot of sense for long-term planning in sports. He had a plan for his years in Oxford and when he was close to world class he extended his plan to break the world record and win the European championships. Had he won an Olympic gold in 1952 (he finished fourth), it seems likely that he would have ended his running career then. After the very successful 1954 season, he finished competitive running at the height of his career. His long-term planning had brought him to the very top. If he had wanted to continue at this level, he would have had to change his training, run more and spend more time on training to keep the same level of competitiveness. This was the time of amateur athletics, and his profession as a doctor was what kept him busy from then onward. [83] To have a long-term plan to reach the top, to progress slowly is good theory. [84]

### *Ergogenic aids*

In his recommendations concerning 'diet', Bannister demonstrates the traditional and 'natural' side of his training. In terms of food, he is not suggesting any medication, vitamins or whatever else had been around in athletics history. Although as a medical student and MD he had access to one of the best medical libraries in the world, he says nothing about ergogenic aids. I am not suggesting that Roger Bannister doped himself, yet in analysing his training it seems quite logical to look not just at the build-up of the engine but also at the fuel. English people are known for the large amount of tea that they drink. A typical hospital routine with long working hours, night shifts and the necessity to train all at the same time can often be maintained only with relatively large amounts of tea or coffee. Each contains caffeine. [85]

In Bannister's time, caffeine was perfectly legal, although it was later placed on the list of prohibited substances by the IOC. At the present time, caffeine is again fully legal. The limit the IOC imposed was well above the amount that had a positive ergogenic effect in events from four to eight minutes: 5–6 mg/kg body mass are considered best for mile running, while the IOC limit of 12 mg/ml urine was to be reached only by 9 mg/kg body mass. [86]

I do not know how much caffeine Bannister was using on the day of his run. It is most likely that he was drinking tea or coffee in doses that had a positive effect, and that had been always been legal.

## Conclusion

When looking at Bannister's training from a modern point of view, it becomes obvious that he was a gifted athlete who applied a relatively modern form of training theory. In his own writing he places considerable emphasis on the mental aspects, rather than the physical. Although this is certainly true, it is not a distinguishing feature of his training in comparison with other successful athletes of any time period. It is very difficult to identify one dominating feature to be *the* factor that determined his success. It is far more likely that the amount of errors made by him from the point of view of training theory was rather limited.

Gunder Hägg basically lived from running – that meant that he ran more often than was reasonable to break the four minutes. Had he been permitted to compete as an amateur a year or even three years longer, he had what it took to break his own world records again. If Bannister is compared with John Landy, his main competitor in 1954, it can be suggested that there is one main reason why Bannister broke the record first and beat Landy in the Commonwealth Games: Landy stated that 'in training I played it very much by ear, and am very much a "train as you feel" man'. [87] So apart from the fact that as a 'front runner' Landy was reluctant to use pacemakers, he was not much of a teamwork man. Although the early Australian season would have favoured him, he was not capable of using two-peak periodization for his purpose. [88]

For other contenders such as Werner Lueg, Rolf Lammers and Josy Barthel, the mile tradition was of minor importance as they had grown up on the metric system. So when they were in top shape, they preferred the metric mile. For Sandor Iharos, 1954 was a year too early. Given Hungarian long-term periodization, he was peaking for the 1956 Olympics. Wes Santee fell victim of the American system at the time, in that he was not capable of competing for his university in the early part of the season. In the second half of the American season, Bannister had already broken the four-minute mile so it is questionable whether Santee was sufficiently motivated.

Bannister was in the tradition that cherished the mile. By acting like a true scientist Bannister used a very modern individualized training, although very often he did not yet have the modern vocabulary to go along with it and make it possible to communicate about it in present-day terms. As can be seen from the information he passed along about his training while he had not yet run his record, he was also quite reluctant to communicate about it at all. [89] But as far as training theory went, his approach was ahead of his time, and there was very little that he did wrong even in modern terms.

## Notes

[1] Announcer Norris McWhirter after Roger Bannister's 'miracle mile' on the Iffley Road track in Oxford on 6 May 1954; see C. Nelson and R. Quercetani, *Runners and races: 1500m./mile* (Los Altos, CA, 1973), p. 118.

[2] Ibid., pp. 94–131.

[3] F. Hoole, *The science and art of training. A handbook for athletes* (London, 1888).

[4] People such as Matveyer in the USSR were first. In the German-language area, D. Harre started his basic textbook as a reader for students of coaching in 1957; see K. Carl, *Training und Trainingslehre in Deutschland* (Schorndorf, 1983), p. 57. Carl looks at Germany only and puts the training for gymnastics and track and field at the centre of his work on the development of the notion of training as a science. He is mainly concerned with general trends in the development of coaching science, independent of the actual context of a particular sport. For differences between East and West Germany at the time, see A. Krüger, 'The preparation of coaches in East and West Germany – Science vs. art', *Newsletter of the International Committee on Comparative Physical Education and Sport*, 2 (1980), pp. 7–15.

[5] R. Bannister, *The first four minutes* (London, 1955).

[6] See C. Chataway, 'Preface' in: F. Stampfl, *Franz Stampfl on running*, 8th edn. (London, 1960), p. 7.

[7] A. Krüger: 'Trainingswissenschaft und Trainingslehre: Kein Text ohne Kontext', *Leistungssport*, 33 (3) (2003), pp. 44–6; A. Krüger: 'Popper, Dewey und die Theorie des Trainings – oder *entscheidend ist auf'n Platz*', *Leistungssport*, 33 (1) (2003), pp. 11–16.

[8] J. Bale, 'Scientific and romantic: The rhetorics of the first four-minute mile', *International Journal of the History of Sport*, 21 (1) (2004), pp. 118–26.

[9] Winning 11 German championships between 1962 and 1976, with best times of 1:47.7 and 3:38.8; coaching athletes to 14 national records, and later working for the elite sport section of the German sports federation, in charge of communication. For the many facets of the terminology, see A. Krüger, 'Mittel- und Langstreckenlauf', in U. Jonath, ed., *Praxis der Leichtathletik* (Berlin, 1973), pp. 87–126.

[10] See e.g. K.L. Popper, *Realism and the aim of science* (London, 1983); K.L. Popper, *The myth of the framework. In defence of science and rationality* (London, 1994).

[11] Bannister, *The first four minutes*, p. 45.

[12] R.G. Bannister, 'The mile', in: H.A. Meyer (ed.), *Track and field athletics* (Letchworth, 1955). Quotes are from the first American edition (New York, 1955), pp. 79–92.

[13] I have used with profit, e.g., R. Parienté, *La fabuleuse histoire de l'athlétisme* (Paris, 1978); there is a long tradition of books such as F. Wilt, *How they train*, vol. 1: *Middle distances*, 2nd edn (Los Altos, CA, 1973). When I look at my own training in there (pp. 98f), I also see the difficulty of describing in a very brief way the actual training; so it may well end up as a mixture of facts and fantasy.

[14] I have been privileged to discuss training theory with some of the finest coaches over the last 45 years, including E. van Aaken, B. Easton, A. Lydiard, M. Igloi,

P.W. Cerutty, J. Bush, B. Sumser, F. Conconi, T. Kepka, F. Horwill, P. Schmidt *et al.* and many international athletes; see e.g. A. Krüger, 'Stand der Trainingslehre zum Mittel- und Langstreckenlauf, Cross-Country und Strassenlauf', *Special Marathon Journal* (1991), pp. 15–17; A. Krüger, 'The History of Middle and Long Distance Running in the Nineteenth and Twentieth Century', in Krüger and A. Teja, eds., *La comune eredità dello sport in Europa. Atti del 1o Seminario Europeo di Storia dello Sport* (Rome, 1997), pp. 117–24; A. Krüger, 'Viele Wege führen nach Olympia. Die Veränderungen in den Trainingssystemen für Mittel- und Langstreckenläufer (1850–1997)', in N. Gissel, ed., *Sportliche Leistung im Wandel* (Hamburg, 1998), pp. 41–56.

[15] G. Smith, *All out for the mile. A history of the mile race, 1864–1955* (London, 1955).

[16] T.S. Kuhn, *The structure of scientific revolutions* (Chicago, 1962).

[17] J. Bale and J. Sang, *Kenyan running: Movement culture, geography and global change* (London, 1996).

[18] P. Nabokov, *Indian running. Native American history and tradition* (Santa Fe, NM, 1987).

[19] Saltin, C.K. Kim, N. Terrados *et al.*, 'Morphology, enzyme activities and buffer capacity in leg muscles of Kenyan and Scandinavian runners', *Scandinavian Journal of Sport Medicine*, 5 (2) (1995), pp. 222–30; V. Billat, P.-M. Lepetre, A.-M. Heugas *et al.*, 'Training and bioenergetic characteristics in elite male and female Kenyan runners', *Med. Sci. Sports Exerc.*, 35 (2) (2003), pp. 297–304; R.A. Scott, E. Georgiades, R.H. Wilson *et al.*, 'Demographic characteristics of elite Ethiopian endurance runners', *Med. Sci. Sports Exerc.*, 10 (35) (2003), pp. 1727–32. My approach is different from A. Roger, 'L'entraînement en athlétisme en France 1919–1973. Une histoire de théoriciens?' (dissertation, Université Lyon I, 2003), for whom the place of the training and the profession of the person who developed a theory determine whether a training is 'scientific' or not. While this structuralist approach might be helpful to explain the struggle within the French athletic scene for supremacy, it is not really helpful to explain Bannister's training.

[20] G. Andrieu, 'Georges Hébert (1875–1957)', in: P. Arnaud, ed., *Le corps en mouvement* (Toulouse, 1981), pp. 291–307; for the long-term effect see Roger, 'L'entraînement', p. 397.

[21] A. Krüger, '"Buying victories is positively degrading": The European origins of government pursuit of national prestige through sports', *International Journal of the History of Sport*, 12 (1995), 201–18; Krüger, '"The Olympic spirit of the modern world has given us a symbol of world war": Sport and national representation at the eve of World War I', in P. Arnaud and A. Wahl, eds., *Sport et rélations internationales* (Centre de Recherche Histoire et Civilisation de l'Université de Metz), 19 (Metz, 1994), pp. 47–64.

[22] For his influence in other countries see: J.-P. Staint-Martin, 'L'oeuvre de George Hébert et son influence à l'étranger: "Nul n'est prophète en son pays"', in *George Hébert. Autour de l'homme et de l'oeuvre* (*Spirales*, 9) (Lyon, 1995), pp. 39–55.

[23] T. Nett, *Bericht über den gemeinsamen IV. Kongress der ITFCA und des III. Kongresses des ELLV. Duisburg 1964* (Berlin, n. d).

[24] J. Murray, 'Alfred A. Shrubb. Champion of the world', in: A.A. Shrubb, *Running and cross country running* (London, 1908), p. 81.

[25] Staged by Pierre de Coubertin in Lausanne, 7–11 May 1913.
[26] M. Hannus, *Finnish running secrets* (Mountain View, CA, 1973).
[27] When running economy is mentioned at all – as in E. Holzer, 'Der Lauf', in E. Holzer, H. Pfeiffer and V. Pimmer, eds., *Lehrbuch der Leichtathletik für Schulen, Sport- und Turnvereine* (Vienna, 1914), p. 31 – it is placed in the context of how to put the feet to the ground properly and thus avoiding muscular aches and pains.
[28] O. Peltzer, *Das Trainingsbuch des Leichtathleten* (Stuttgart, 1926), p. 167.
[29] M. Brustmann, *Olympisches Trainierbuch*, 2nd edn (Berlin, 1920), pp. 53f (in this respect no difference from the 1st edn, 1912).
[30] This is stressed by the emphasis on stylistically proper running, see e.g. R. Koch, *Der Lauf* (Leipzig, 1927).
[31] Ibid., pp. 29–33.
[32] P. de Coubertin, 'La réprise des traveaux du Congrès de Lausanne', *Bulletin du BIPS*, 1 (1) (1929), pp. 6–14.
[33] P. de Coubertin, *Leçons de gymnastique utilitaire. Sauvetage-Défence – Locomotion* (Paris, 1916), p. 6.
[34] J. Germain and A. Willemet, 'Le sport et l'intelligence. Grande enquête sur l'avenir et la nécessité du sport en France', *La Révue Mondiale*, 151 (22), pp. 131–51; (23), pp. 259–72; (24), pp. 445–56 (all 1922): the quote is from P. de Coubertin, p. 147.
[35] G. Harbig, *Unvergessener Rudolf Harbig* (Berlin, 1956).
[36] T. Nett, *Training des Kurz-, Mittel- und Langstreckenläufers* (Frankfurt/M, 1954), pp. 55–71.
[37] L. Pihkala, *Allgemeine Richtlinien für das athletische Training* (Berlin, 1931); this is an offprint of the chapter in C. Krümmel, ed., *Athletik* (Berlin, 1930).
[38] W. Gerschler, *Harbigs Aufstieg zum Weltrekord* (Dresden, 1939). Internationally the Gerschler method was also applied partially by F. Stampfl, *Franz Stampfl on running*, 8th edn (London, 1960).
[39] G. Pirie, *Running wild* (London, 1961).
[40] C. Nelson, *The Jim Ryun story* (Los Altos, CA, 1967).
[41] R. Donath, *Mittelstrecken- und Hindernislauf* (East Berlin, 1960), pp. 10ff.
[42] G. Hägg, *So brach ich Weltrekorde* (Nürnberg, 1949); P. Brie, *Gunder Hägg. Vom Holzfäller zum Weltrekordler* (Murten: Pro Leichtathletik, 1948). The French success of M. Jazy and M. Bernard later was based on a similar system. They even went to train in Sweden on their original training ground in Valadalen.
[43] A. Krüger, 'Mihaly Igloi. The man and the system', in *Runners' World* (ed.), *Guide to distance running* (Mountain View, CA, 1969), p. 168.
[44] A. Lydiard and G. Gilmore, *Run to the top* (London, 1962).
[45] H. Mittenzwei, 'Grundlagen, Mittel und Methoden des Ausdauertrainings für die Vorbereitung unserer Sportler auf die Olympischen Spiele 1964', in Forschungsstelle der DHfK, Brigade Ausdauertraining, ed., *Ausdauertraining im Leistungssport* (Leipzig, 1964), pp. 12ff. For the link between training and racing, see A. Krüger, 'Periodization or peaking at the right time', *Track Technique*, 54 (1974), pp. 1720–4.
[46] See e.g. the official publication of the BAAB, D.C.V. Watts and H. Wilson, *Middle and long distance, marathon and steeplechase* (London, 1973), pp. 20ff.

[47] B. Bowerman, 'The Oregon school of running', in T.P. Rosandich, ed., *Track in theory and technique* (Hollywood, CA: 1962), p. 147. The same can be said about later Oregon runners such as the unforgettable Pre; for a more extensive approach see B. Dellinger and B. Freeman, *The competitive runner's training book* (New York, 1984).
[48] J. Hoberman, *Mortal engines. The science of performance and the dehumanization of Sport* (New York, 1992), p. 94.
[49] D.L. Costill, *A scientific approach to distance running* (Palo Alto, CA, 1979).
[50] A. Krüger, 'Nachwort über den neusten Stand der Literatur zur Periodisierung', in L.P. Matwejew, ed., *Periodisierung des sportlichen Trainings* (Berlin, 1972), pp. 201–31.
[51] P. W. Cerutty, *Athletics. How to become a champion*, 6th edn (London, 1963).
[52] M. Bernard, *La rage de courir. 25 ennées de courses à pied* (Paris, 1975). This was quite in contrast to the very physiological French training, e.g. J.R. Lacour, 'Étude physiologique de la course à pied', in C. Dessons, G. Drut *et al.*, eds., *Les courses* (Paris, 1982), pp. 7–76. For the dispute in France see Roger, 'L'entraînement', pp. 384–401.
[53] P. Falk, *The consuming body* (London, 1994); C. Shilling, *The body and social theory* (London, 1993); J. Friedman, *Cultural identity and global process* (London, 1994).
[54] A. dal Monte, M. Faina *et al.*, 'Il consumo massimo d'ossigeno in telemetria', *Revista di Cultura Sportiva*, 8 (15) (1989), pp. 35–44.
[55] M. Reiss and U. Pfeiffer, eds., *Leistungsreserven im Sport* (Berlin, 1991).
[56] J.K. Doherty, *Modern track and field*, 2nd edn (Englewood Cliffs, NJ, 1960), p. 165.
[57] R.J. Shephard and P.O. Åstrand, eds., *Endurance in Sport* (1992).
[58] Bannister, 'The mile', pp. 86–8.
[59] G. Smith, *All out for the mile* (London, 1955); Bannister, *The first four minutes*.
[60] K.A. Ericsson, R.T. Krampe and C. Tesch-Römer, 'The role of deliberate practice in the acquisition of expert performance', *Psychological Review*, 100 (1993), pp. 363–406.
[61] J.L. Starkes and K.A. Ericsson, eds., *Expert performances in sports. Advances in research on sport expertise* (Champaign, IL, 2003).
[62] For his youthful and long-term approaches, see J. Bale, *Roger Bannister and the four-minute mile* (London, 2004).
[63] Bannister, 'The mile', p. 88.
[64] Bale, 'Scientific and romantic', p. 123.
[65] See A. Lydiard, *Run the Lydiard way* (London, 1978), pp. 72–6.
[66] Stampfl, *Franz Stampfl on running*, p. 27.
[67] Lydiard, *Run the Lydiard way*, p. 73; for the (neuro)physiological side see P.V. Komi, 'The stretch-shortening cycle and the human power output', in N.L. Jones, N. McCartney and A.J. McComas, eds., *Human muscle power* (Champaign, IL, 1986), pp. 27–40.
[68] Bannister, *The first four minutes*, p. 171.
[69] Nett, *Training des Kurz-, Mittel- und Langstreckenläufers*, p. 254.
[70] Donath, *Mittelstrecken- und Hindernislauf*, pp. 142ff.
[71] Bannister, *The first four minutes*, p. 89.
[72] Ibid., p. 85.

[73] Stampfl, *Franz Stampfl on running*, pp. 111–16.

[74] G. Schnabel, D. Harre and A. Borde, eds., *Trainingswissenschaft. Leistung – Training – Wettkampf* (Berlin, 1994), pp. 353ff.; R.W. Stremel, 'Historical development of the anaerobic threshold concept', *Physiologist*, 27 (1984), pp. 295–98; W.L. Kenney and J.L. Hodgson, 'Variables predictive of performance in elite middle-distance runners', *Journal of Biomechanics*, 32 (5) (1999), pp. 461–5; A.J. Ward-Smith, 'The bioenergetics of optimal performances in middle-distance and long-distance track running', *British Journal of Sports Medicine*, 19 (4) (1985), pp. 207–9; P. Janssen, *Lactate Threshold Training* (Champaign, IL, 2001).

[75] For the Soviet training theorist M.J. Nabatnikowa, *Die spezielle Ausdauer des Sportlers* (Berlin, 1974), p. 74, these $10 \times 400$ m are ideal test runs.

[76] Schnabel, Harre and Borde, *Trainingswissenschaft*, p. 58.

[77] Bale, *Roger Bannister*, p. 68.

[78] For a more recent application see A. Krüger, 'Nachwort über den neusten Stand der Literatur zur Periodisierung', in L.P. Matwejew, *Periodisierung des sportlichen Trainings* (Berlin, 1972), pp. 201–31; Krüger, 'Periodization or peaking'.

[79] W. H. Freeman, *Peak when it counts: Periodization for American track and field* (Los Altos, CA, 1989); T.O. Bompa, *Periodization: Theory and methodology of training* (Champaign, IL, 1999).

[80] Schnabel, Harre and Borde, *Trainingswissenschaft,* p. 87.

[81] P. Tschiene, 'Wettkampfvorbereitung und Wettkämpfe in den Laufdisziplinen der Leichtathletik', in G. Thiess and P. Tschiene, eds., *Handbuch zur Wettkampflehre* (Aachen, 1999); pp. 199–207.

[82] Bannister, *The first four minutes*, p. 45.

[83] For the question of social capital as potential gain in amateur times see Bale, *Roger Bannister*.

[84] Schnabel, Harre and Borde, *Trainingswissenschaft*, pp. 442–4.

[85] S. Reents, 'Caffeine', in Reents, *Sport and exercise pharmacology* (Champaign, IL, 2000), pp. 277–96; L.L. Spriet, 'Caffeine', in M.S. Bahrke and C.E. Yesalis, eds., *Performance enhancing substances in sport and exercise* (Champaign, IL, 2002), pp. 267–78; M.H. Williams, 'Caffeine', in *The ergogenic edge* (Champaign, IL, 1998), pp. 149–53.

[86] A. Krüger, 'Doping and the ethics of sport in post-modern societies', in A. Daino, ed., *Sport – Ethics – Cultures. Human Rights – Society-Olympic Movement*, vol. 1 (Rapallo, 2004), pp. 99–116; Krüger, 'Anmerkungen zur historischen und ethischen Dimension von Doping und Dopingforschung', *Beiträge zur Sportgeschichte*, 7 (1998), pp. 45–58; Krüger, 'Die Paradoxien des Dopings – ein Überblick', in M. Gamper, J. Mühlethaler and F. Reidhaar, eds., *Doping – Spitzensport als gesellschaftliches Problem* (Zürich, 2000), pp. 11–33. Running for 240 seconds, the expected improvement of between 1 and 2 per cent would make 2.4 to 4.8 seconds for a one-mile run.

[87] Quoted in Wilt, *How they train*, vol. 1, p. 102.

[88] Krüger, 'Periodization or peaking'.

[89] Bale, *Roger Bannister*, p. 57.

# Habitus, Barriers and the [Ab]use of the Science of Interval Training in the 1950s

P. David Howe

This contribution highlights the tension between rival schools of thought, embodied in two coaches, regarding the most effective approach to training athletes in the middle-distance running events during the 1950s. Exploring the methods used by Franz Stampfl and Percy Wells Cerutty to help their athletes break the barrier of the first four-minute mile, the paper will attempt to unravel some of the myths surrounding the training of great athletes in the 1950s and their relationships with these men. The training of Stampfl has long been regarded as cold and scientific, whereas the methods of Cerutty relied on a tacit knowledge of the body derived from the use of a distinctive training philosophy – the creed of the

'Stotan'. In effect the 'battle' between the two coaches was seen to be ideological. However, a close examination of the methods employed by both Stampfl and Cerutty highlights that they largely relied upon similar methods, methods that developed embodied habit, and it was simply where the training took place that was in fact distinct.

The training methods of Franz Stampfl, the adviser to Roger Bannister, and Percy Cerutty, adviser, teacher and/or mentor of John Landy and Herb Elliot, still have resonance today in the preparation of elite middle- and long-distance runners. While today's training sessions of the elite are riddled with new training 'fads' designed to enhance performance, the root of most contemporary training is derived from the successful training regimes developed by these coaches. In the context of the 50th anniversary of the four-minute mile, attention has focused on older methods of training, i.e. those that pre-dated the 1950s, which facilitated that great achievement. [1] This paper will demonstrate that while Stampfl and Cerutty appeared to use distinctive training methods, they actually shared a fundamental principle. [2] The bodies of the elite runners were put through their paces in order that the act of training should become habitual, facilitating a conditioning effect that would allow the athlete to run at fast pace for longer. A conceptual framework related to the concept of habit adopted by both Bourdieu [3] and Merleau-Ponty [4] will be used to show how the distinct approaches to training can lead to the same outcome – a world-beating athlete. Habits created through training that require a disciplined body can be seen to be fundamental to a training environment that is conducive to achieving great performances. [5]

The coaches came to the training of elite athletes from different angles. Cerutty was a relatively successful athlete in his native Australia. His training approaches were fashioned after his own trial and error, which was a result of being rather sickly in his youth. [6] Stampfl on the other hand appears to have been a character whose understanding of the necessity of training was the product of a more traditional scientific knowledge of the body but also a strong desire to relate to and befriend the athletes with whom he worked. [7]

The data on which this analysis of training is based are by their very nature secondary – simply because the art of training elite athletes has never been an exact science. Several key texts have been used to help piece together an understanding of methods employed by the coaches who were 'behind' the key protagonists in the race for the four-minute mile. By scrutinizing the literature that has been published by these coaches as well as some of the books that have been published by and/or on their star athletes, it is hoped that this paper will illuminate an understanding of the art of coaching in the 1950s. [8] As Arthur Lydiard, a coach who received worldwide acclaim in 1960 following the success of athletes trained by him at the Rome Olympics, most notably Peter Snell and Murray Halberg, and who would have been well versed in the methods of Stampfl and Cerutty, suggests, 'coaching distance-runners is like assembling a jigsaw', and this paper will attempt to show how Stampfl and Cerutty each put together the puzzle correctly using distinctive training methods. [9]

Before examining the training methods employed by each coach, however, it is important to provide an outline of the social concept of habit because both Stampfl and Cerutty used this formation to ingrain their athletes with the key skills that can be developed from their training methods. After an examination of the training methods of the two coaches the paper will turn to a discussion regarding the value of using habit and its embodied manifestation, disposition, to better interpret the training methods of these coaches.

## The habit of training

In order to fully appreciate the art and science of coaching associated with elite middle-distance running in the 1950s, the concept of embodiment needs to be brought into the analysis. Kimayer has suggested that

> The anthropological use of the metaphor of embodiment serves to maintain a place for the richness of bodily experience and significance of bodies as agents and areas of action. Embodiment works against the tendency to treat bodies simply as property (my body and yours) or as vehicles entirely subordinate to our will. The essential insight of embodiment is that the body has a life of its own and that social worlds become inscribed on, or sedimented in, body physiology, habitus, and experience. [10]

From a methodological perspective, embodiment postulates that the body is not an object to be studied in relation to the cultural world but is the subject of culture or the existential ground of culture. [11] In particular this paper adopts an embodied approach to explore the habits imposed upon the elite middle-distance runners who were under the watchful eyes of the coaches who are central to this paper. The adoption of habitual training of the body can be seen to be central to much of the work that has been done, past and present, examining the body in the social world. [12] The examination of habit illuminates the concept of agency as important to a practical and embodied praxis. In other words the physical manifestation of culture through embodied action is fundamental to exploring the importance of the body in the context of training regimes within the sport of athletics.

Physical action that becomes embodied in certain situations may be seen as habitual and these acts are often drilled into an athlete through countless repetitions that lack imagination. This can take the form of kicking drills in football or sprinting drills in track and field, for example. Habitual acts that are further developed by improvisation can be considered dispositions. [13] A disposition is an underlying tendency or propensity to act in a certain way and therefore is more flexible than the habits that result from the learning of rudimentary drills. However, a disposition is still achieved without conscious thought before the action. The disposition is the embodied ability to put the habitual training together in such a way that it can be quickly adapted to suit any situation. Our disposition will suggest that we are likely act in a certain way given a particular social situation. This distinction between habit and disposition is useful in that it explores the notion of human intervention in the sporting environment. When an athlete goes through the training regime required of an elite middle-distance runner, his or her body habitually knows what the 'race-pace' is simply by the 'feel' of the body: there is no need to rely upon a stopwatch. Changes that occur within a race in terms of the tactics of the other competitors and the ability of the athlete to respond are directly linked to the disposition or the ability to improvise that the athlete innately has developed through physical training and lived experiences more generally.

Merleau-Ponty's conceptualization of corporeal schema is of importance when trying to determine how athletes (and other actors) make the decisions they do without really thinking about them. [14] When athletes make a strategic move in a race, they do not have to think about running or accelerating; in a sense they 'know without knowing'. According to Crossley, 'the corporeal schema is an incorporated bodily know-how and practical sense; a perspectival grasp upon the world from the "point of view" of the body'. [15] Corporeal schema therefore, and the embodied knowledge that it entails, needs to be excavated in order to establish how the coaches at the heart of the research were able to train athletes to perform at the highest level.

Merleau-Ponty's concept of corporeal schema articulates nicely the embodied agency of a runner both as an individual and as a member of the social environment surrounding sporting contests. [16] The corporeal schema comprises the skills required for the performance and the practical understanding of the race that may be transformed depending on the action of other runners. A good runner reads a race without thinking. In other words, he/she explores the relationship between different levels of structure that constrict movement at a subconscious level.

Commenting on the work of Merleau-Ponty Crossley suggests:

> Habit involves a modification and enlargement of the corporeal schema, an incorporation of new 'principles' of action and know-how, which permit new ways of acting and understanding. It is a sediment of past activity which remains alive in the present in the form of the structures of corporeal schema; shaping perception, conception, deliberation, emotion and action. [17]

In fact the emphasis on innovation gives the runner the raw material to turn into habit. [18] As a result, innovative habits that are a product of creative praxis result in a diachronic shift in the social world.

For Bourdieu, an athlete's habitus is the embodied sediment of every encounter he or she has had with the social world. [19] It can be used in the present to mould perception, thought and action to the extent that it has an important role to play in decisions that an agent might make in future encounters. In this sense actors in general and, in the case of this research, elite middle-distance runners who are manipulated by coaches specifically can be seen not simply to follow rules but also to bend them in much the same way as Merleau-Ponty conceptualizes improvisation as being fundamental to an individual's disposition. [20] Dispositions, or more generally forms of social competence, may be seen as a product of well-established social environments. It may have been a disposition that Stampfl was referring to here:

> Training is principally an act of faith. The athlete must believe in its efficacy; he must believe that through training he will become fitter and stronger; that by constant repetition of the same movements he will become more skilful and his muscles more relaxed. He must believe that through training his performance will improve and continue to improve indefinitely for as long as he continues to train to progressively stiffer standard. He must be a fanatic for hard work and enthusiastic enough to enjoy it. [21]

Every action of an athlete embodies a structure and logic that is distinctive to the game and level at which it is played. As such, the work of Merleau-Ponty [22] and that of Bourdieu [23] are useful allies. In other words, while society may be seen as shaping agents, it needs individuals' improvisations from time to time if it is going to evolve. Therefore in the 1950s world of middle-distance training, it is as important to see the body as a product of the self as much as it is of society. It is the self that provides improvisation by drawing upon the sediment of previous social encounters. This is evident when a sporting contest is observed. While the event is run within a set of rules (any transgressors ideally are penalized) a sporting performance is full of improvisation, much like good jazz. [24] Some sports are more dependent than others on improvisation. In middle-distance running, improvisation in the form of a change in racing strategy can be beneficial, whereas in figure skating it is not.

The ability to improvise is an important quality to embrace when an athlete is being educated in the embodied habits of an elite middle-distance runner. Abrahams in the early 1950s suggests that 'training is that process of education of the body which prepares it to meet with safety exceptional and extreme demands upon its energy'. [25] This view of training then could be seen as an appropriate backdrop against which to examine the training methods adopted by two of the leading coaches in the British Empire in the 1950s.

## Franz Stampfl

The debate as to whether Franz Stampfl was actually the coach of Roger Bannister during the epic summer of 1954 may never be settled. Certainly, in his own account of this remarkable season, Bannister refers to Stampfl as the coach of his good friends Chris Brasher and Chris Chataway. [26] Commenting in the foreword to Stampfl's treatise *On running*, Bannister hints strongly at their close relationship:

> I have had the opportunity of seeing him at work and of discussing some of my own racing problems with him. He has been with me at the time of critical races and indeed, in the last year, his counsel has often helped me to defeat formidable opponents on the track. [27]

The reason Bannister may have played down the role of Stampfl in his success may have been his desire to adopt the amateur virtues of a gentleman. To be seen to require help in the achievement of success on the athletics track goes against the traditional ideals of the Oxbridge life. Bale, in his recent book evaluating 50 years of the four-minute mile, has shown that beneath the Oxford veneer Bannister was not what would be considered a 'gentleman' (of the *Chariots of Fire* type) in post-war Britain. [28] Bannister's denial of Stampfl as a coach may be considered residual nostalgia for the bygone days of athletics that he himself, through his physiological experiments, was placing in the past. [29]

Whether or not Stampfl 'coached' Bannister during the final few seasons of his athletic career, it is clear that the philosophy Stampfl brought to the track would have left the door open for Bannister to seek advice as and when it was needed. In the final chapter of *On running*, which is entitled 'The coach's job', Stampfl states:

> Not all athletes feel the need for full-time coaching. Some prefer to work out their own destinies and do so both intelligently and successfully. Sooner or later it sometimes occurs that they are faced by some problem on which they need independent advice, and at such moments the coach can be of true practical assistance. [30]

This statement suggests a man who was happy to be of assistance as and when athletes might need his knowledge. It also implies that Stampfl was far from being the science-obsessed coach that might correspond with Bannister's experimentation. [31] As Chris Chataway suggests,

> For Franz Stampfl athletics presents an exciting challenge – a different and personal challenge to each individual, no matter what may be his initial capabilities. It is something to be taken in a spirit of adventure; and success is the reward, not only for physical condition, but also for quick thinking, intelligent planning, and the courage to risk more in the race than any of the opposition. [32]

Stampfl himself echoes these remarks:

> The important thing is that the coach should be available to all, giving of his experience whenever it is required. By so doing he does himself a service. By making himself available to all and sundry, his knowledge of human nature is broadened by his many contacts, his eyes are sharpened by constant practice and his experience deepens. In fact he becomes a better coach. [33]

While Stampfl may have made himself available to all those who asked for his help, it is clear that his methods of coaching, with their personal touch, were tied to a scientific application, not so much in the form of experimentation but rather connected to his reliance on the seasonality of training and an overall reliance upon time in the final stages of preparation. [34] The Stampfl regime began in the autumn, when a period of time was spent doing easy cross-country running, which was felt to place the least demands upon the athlete. This period would be followed by the use of *fartlek*, a Swedish word that literally means speed play. Here runners would engage in steady running interspersed with much faster running over undulating countryside. [35] This stage would help create in the body the habit of running fast with minimal recovery. Fartlek was certainly a more intense stage of the development cycle, but this was followed by interval training, which could be seen as replicating in a more scientific way the benefits that result from training using the methods of *fartlek*.

Interval training, as Stampfl conducted it. took place on a measured track of 440 yards or 400 metres. Repetitions could be conducted over any measured distance with this standardized track. If Stampfl's middle-distance charges were asked to carry out intervals over 440 yards after each effort, a lap of the track would be jogged in three minutes before the next effort was undertaken. This might be repeated ten times, with the time required for each effort being fixed based on the athlete's current potential. Over time – say, a period of a month or so – the 'rest interval' for the jogged lap might be reduced as the athlete's stamina improved. Simply put, a fast lap of the track should be followed by a slow one, but the importance of this type of workout is that 'The recovery run must always be long enough and slow enough for the athlete to recover normal breathing and to recover from fatigue. The recovery time is customarily two-and-a-half to three times as long as that of the last lap, but with increased fitness this should decrease steadily.' [36] The flexibility of interval training is the key to its long-standing success as a method currently employed in similar forms by coaches around the world today. Interval training 'induces speed and stamina – which together produce pace – pace-judgement and an all-round improvement in physical well-being'. [37]

The penultimate stage of the Stampfl method is repetition running. This is where athletes run distances usually no more than half the length of the race. For milers such as Bannister this would be 880 yards:

> The predetermined speed at which each half-mile is to be run will, of course, be governed by the ability of the athlete; and the period of rest by his physical fitness. The important point to remember is that the rest must be long enough to allow the man to return to normal breathing and recover from fatigue. Every run must be accurately timed, in the course of which the athlete has further opportunity for checking and adjusting his judgement of pace. [38]

By the time that Stampfl's athletes were able to handle repetition running they would be close to having the physical fitness to engage in a time trial up to several weeks before a competitive outing. Bannister used this approach before his historic mile run in Oxford, running over three-quarters of a mile in under three minutes on 24 April 1954. Two days later, he ran a half-mile in 1:54, which gave him and those around him confidence in his ability to break four minutes for the mile.

For the later part of the training that Stampfl's athletes engaged in, a stopwatch was a vital part of the training process. Without one, an athlete would not be able to objectively measure his progress in training and be able to 'see' speed habits forming that are vital in the achievement of goals. Commenting on the fundamentals of athletics, Stampfl suggests:

> Interval and repetition running, which have their being centred in accurate timing, cannot exist without a stop-watch [*sic*] and on them rests the athlete's main means of acquiring the race-winning quality, which we call pace-judgement. Sense of pace can only come from experience gained from repeated runs over the same distance in the same time. [39]

But it is important here that Stampfl is clear that the use of a stopwatch is not simply a tool of science but has a role to play in developing enthusiasm that to him is key to the development of an athlete:

> Of almost equal importance is the stop-watch's psychological value. It keeps the athlete's interest alive by turning what would otherwise be guess-work into facts and figures. During the training period before the competitive season begins it supplies much of the incentive to perseverance that otherwise comes only from racing itself. [40]

This praise of the stopwatch is distinctive to the attitude and approach of another great coach of this era, Percy Wells Cerutty, to whom this paper will now turn.

## Percy Wells Cerutty

Like for Franz Stampfl, who had guided first Roger Bannister to the four-minute mile and then later that year Chris Chataway to a world record over 5,000 metres, 1954 was also a success for the coaching methods of Percy Wells Cerutty. He played at least some part in guiding John Landy to a mile world record of 3 minutes 57.9 seconds, only 46 days after Bannister had broken the four-minute barrier. Though his charge had finished second at the Empire Games of that year, this made the athletics world take note of his training methods as a valuable way in which to build a champion middle-distance runner.

Unlike Stampfl, Cerutty had his own ambitions as an athlete and remained a competitive athlete until 11 November 1950, when he was 55 years old. [41] It was only then that he turned his attention to coaching full-time. His dictum was simply 'If you can't do it, you can't teach it'. [42]

Cerutty in fact did not like being referred to as a coach, in part because to him the athlete needs to be shown the way to the top by a teacher:

> Success, the getting to the top is a technique: a philosophy. I teach just that. And the principal factor, as I understand it, is not to say do this or that, but to show the way; to be able to draw upon one's own experiences; to be able to enter the personality of the person who would learn; to be able to hearten and enthuse, as well as suggest new techniques; new approaches, new aims and goals. [43]

Cerutty's approach to his training methods was outlined in his own creed: 'The creed of the Stotan was formed from the stoic, who was unmoved by joy or grief; and one who submits without complaint to unavoidable necessity; and Spartans, who were hardy and undaunted.' [44] This approach to training was a philosophy that blended common sense and logic with principles of strength and endurance that allowed for the development of good people and, often, great athletes. The most important point that his charges had to follow was 'to give wholehearted loyalty, obedience and support to the leader'. [45] This approach to training was developed through a process of trial and error that took ten years to fully develop and a great deal of emphasis was placed upon running style. Cerutty spent his time when he was not training himself thoroughly researching the movements of graceful members of the animal kingdom in order to develop a better understanding of how a champion athlete should move.

> Athletes should run with relaxed power, grace and resilience as well as the proud but controlled movement of the racehorse, the upness, the feeling of being over the ground that the gazelle demonstrates, the litheness and ferocity of the leopard, and to have the maturity that is evinced in the lion. [46]

The desire to study animal movement is part of the creed that highlights getting back to nature. It has been suggested that Cerutty's training may be seen as 'athletic anthropology' since, as well as focusing upon animal movement, he was also intrigued by the running styles of indigenous people. [47] This might be part of the reason he set up his rural retreat in order that he and his athletes could get away from the urban environment of Melbourne, which he may have felt was responsible for his decline in health during the mid 1940s – though this point is never made explicitly. [48] Staple running routes around Cerutty's Portsea training base, 60 miles south of Melbourne, were running repeats around an undulating golf course and attacking a sand hill that was 80 feet high and rated 1:1.5. Training also included weightlifting but was largely unstructured. The athletes were encouraged to undertake training under the principles of the creed following the examples of their enthusiastic mentor, who believed in an ethos of rewards for hard work that would create the habits and dispositions of a champion:

> The athletes who imagined that I would personally supervise their training were soon disillusioned. They were expected to keep a diary of their daily training, their results and opinions. I never asked to see one. They were all told what was essential to get to the top. Those who had not the will, then, to work out their own schedule, to test and try for themselves, I looked upon as deficient in the main factors, initiative, self-induced drives and intelligence. [49]

Athletes were therefore to follow Cerutty's lead when it came to training by taking in the lessons he had taught and moulding them personally to their own situation. Dietary advice was an area where Cerutty has had an impact on training today through the way he articulates this information. In spite of his protestations to the contrary, this advice is somewhat mechanical or even pseudo-scientific:

> We are not soul, or brain, or thinking substance, we are bones and meat and blood. And this is made from the food we eat, the fluids that are drunk and the air that is inhaled. Poor materials can make only poor buildings and adulterated foods cannot be expected to produce the best results. [50]

Such evidence flies in the face of Cerutty's public discourse of being opposed to a scientific approach. Privately he clearly believed in a scientific approach to training, evinced both in his conceptualization of nutrition and in his use of interval training and the stopwatch. Cerutty and Franz Stampfl [51] discussed their respective theories of training in the Olympic Village in Helsinki in 1952. According to Cerutty, they agreed on little when it came to what is important in training elite middle distance runners:

> So Franz Stampfl and myself both went our own ways, teaching in our own ways, myself with the emphasis on technique, Franz on the importance of tracks, and the personality of the coach. Add to this the 'Interval System,' first enunciated by the Germans, under the aegis of Professor Gerschler, and my own preference for the Fartlek system of the great Swedish coach, Goster Holmer. [52]

The interval training system requires the use of a stopwatch to which Cerutty claims he is opposed, yet a picture plate in a volume on his life shows (and reads) 'A shot of Don MacMillan and John Landy *being timed* by Percy Cerutty in a training workout at the Portsea Oval before the 1952 Olympic Games'. [53] This, together with the details of training undertaken by John Landy during the same period, clearly highlighting intervals conducted over varying distances, must be considered proof positive that he had adopted the use of a stopwatch. [54] Yet in order that his training creed would remain intact, he continued to advocate training based on more natural circumstances. Kelly quotes Cerutty as saying the following:

> The academic coaches use stopwatches and assume that the psyche is nothing, and that instinct cannot be trusted. Such concepts as the rigid schedule, the worked-out and the laid-down day-by-day training routines, find no sympathy with me, or my ideas. Despite the efforts of the industrialist, we are still humans, not machines. [55]

This statement may reflect the bitterness that Cerutty felt towards Stampfl, who was appointed to a full-time coaching post in Cerutty's home state of Victoria, Australia. So blinkered are his attitudes, perhaps hardened by a clash of personality, that it is clear Cerutty believes that Stampfl's system is entirely mechanistic and therefore of no long-term benefit to the personality of an athlete:

> Such mechanical, stereotyped and regimented form of training – unimaginative and lacking of joy – can have no common denominator with the concept of amateur athleticism and the freezing of the whole personality. Rather they must make for the conditioned response, the treadmill means to a dubious objective as far as the personality of the athlete is concerned. And this is true whether a coach sets a formalized plan or the athlete conspires to set his own. The damage to the personality will be the same. There must be no set schedule, no daily direction that is fixed and pre-calculated. Nothing at all that is rigidly based on authority, whether imposed from within or without. [56]

It must be remembered here that Cerutty, as earlier mentioned, expected his charges to follow his lead in terms of the manner in which they conducted their training in relation to the creed of the Stotan. When an athlete took it upon himself to not follow the teachings of Cerutty, as was the case with John Landy towards the end of his career, he was charged with being arrogant. [57]

Cerutty's desire to achieve success through the use of his 'natural' training methods did not stop him from continuing to adapt his system to the rigours of modern-day athletics fine tuning the habit forming potential the programme. His criticisms of athletes who do not follow his creed to the letter may have been unfounded, for he never outlined a training programme in the manner of Stampfl. Cerutty never gave them a schedule of any sort between their visits to his training camp at Portsea. [58]

> No schedules are set at the camp and everyone has to think for himself, but they all know what is expected from them while they are at the camp. The old master drives himself around the track, or up the sandhill, or over a gruelling circuit to demonstrate what is expected, and how, or perhaps to shame an athlete, . . . into producing a superior effort. The ones who succeed learn to have courage, persistence and an inurement to pain and suffering. [59]

This approach to training, by today's standards, appears haphazard and yet Cerutty knew that athletes needed to use everything at their disposal in order to win. He felt the training that his athletes engaged in was sufficient, especially considering that he felt the psychological component was a 'natural' element of the training process:

> In the game of athletics, especially on a world-class level, just as in politics, business and national ambitions, the game is played hard, and few or any punches pulled. We are all out to win. Not only win but win at all costs. Anyone that thinks otherwise must be considered amongst the simple. It is true, winning at all cost does not mean breaking the rules, but every means open to athletes and coaches are used, naturally, mostly psychologically. [60]

It is interesting that Cerutty feels the use of psychology is a 'natural' part of the preparation and that this sort of preparation can be untaken by those who coach the athletes. Despite his dislike for the approach to coaching of Stampfl, if he had actually sat down and read Stampfl's *On running* closely he would have been aware of the importance that was placed on psychology. [61] In the current environment surrounding high-performance sport the use of a trained sport psychologist is commonplace, yet their interventions are not directly part of the coaching process and are seen as inherently scientific.

Cerutty continued to advocate a training that was not based on standardization or the use of a stopwatch, and yet details of the programmes his athletes actually engaged in suggest otherwise. The training of Herb Elliott, which was to have taken a natural approach, highlights an interest in interval training similar to that openly advocated by Stampfl. [62] The importance of the natural environment and the unstructured, self-prescribed routines of the athletes that followed the stotan creed and the success they derived from their involvement from Percy Cerutty is hard to argue against. Both John Landy and Herb

Elliott were great milers, but it was Cerutty's belief that it the natural element of the programmes that he set for his charges that prepared them best:

> The naturalness of the life and environment, the unsophisticated atmosphere and the resistance of the training routes, or the weight-lifting and the spirited opposition from training rivals, is responsible for developing a stronger man. It is not just the training that is secondary. It is the battle against oneself, and the man who can battle the hardest and torture his body the most who will most succeed. [63]

In this brief description of the methods employed by Percy Cerutty, I have argued that he was not as opposed to the method of interval training as he would have liked the athletic world to believe. This observation comes partly from a privileged position of someone who, through a 25-year involvement in middle- and long-distance running, understands the methods of training that are commonly adopted today and which do not make a distinction between the places or sites of training and the methods employed. In the following section an attempt will be made to highlight the similarities in the methods of Stampfl and Cerutty before a tentative conclusion is reached.

## Discussion

The methods employed by Franz Stampfl and Percy Cerutty in the training of elite middle-distance runners were linked because they were involved in the preparation of two of the leading protagonists in the quest for the first four-minute mile. After Bannister's success at Oxford in 1954 in breaking the four-minute barrier, albeit in a paced race, and then importantly against a Cerutty-influenced John Landy, by then the holder of the mile world record, at the Empire Games in Vancouver during July the same year, Stampfl's methods were in the ascendant. [64] It transpired later that Landy had not followed the advice of Cerutty, which was not to lead. Landy blamed him for ruining his preparation before the 1952 Olympic Games, an event in which he was eliminated in the heats. [65] In the 'miracle mile', as the race at the Empire Games was christened, Landy had taken the lead at the end of the first lap and had ultimately played into the hands of the fast-finishing Bannister – immortalized in the picture of Landy glancing left for Bannister, who was already level with the Australian around the final bend. [66]

The success of the Stampfl-advised Bannister over Cerutty-advised Landy might have laid the foundation for the state of Victoria (Australia), where Cerutty resided, selecting Stampfl as its full-time athletics coach. While Cerutty suggests this was not a problem for him, he devoted considerable time to discussing a general lack of respect for Stampfl's methods and implies that many Australians wanted him to have the full-time post. [67] This of course could be one of the reasons why Cerutty was so opposed to the methods of Stampfl and why, as mentioned previously, he was so openly against what he perceived to be the scientization of training. The local press in Australia caught on to the different schools of thought as regards training and the *Melbourne Sun* reporter Jack Dunn wrote in 1957:

> Cerutty spurns the repetition training advocated by Franz Stampfl and followed successfully by Merv Lincoln. The vastly different methods of Stampfl and Cerutty will be thoroughly tested when Elliott and Lincoln clash during the summer season. Both coaches believe that they are right and are determined to prove their points, so their rivalry could produce benefits, in the form of high running standards and more records for Australian athletics. [68]

In spite of the spectacle created, in part by the media, in relation to the different training methods used by the two coaches, it can be argued that the training methods were *not* particularly distinct.

Both Stampfl and Cerutty adopted training methods, like coaches before them, that established a habitual response in their athletes. The physical act of training, regardless of where and how it is carried out, produces a sporting body that is tuned in to certain habits. The difference in their approaches was not the use of scientific training but rather the geographical space where the training took place. Much of Stampfl's system was based upon the value associated with interval training, which requires an accurate measurement not so much of the distance covered in each effort – though this is important – but rather the length of rest taken between each effort. The same effect can be developed through the use of a strenuous hill, such as the one used at Portsea by Cerutty, which creates an environment where the body is pushed so as to resist stopping. Easy running back down the hill creates an interval rest in much the same way as the jog recoveries undertaken by Stampfl's athletes around their track.

What is distinct, therefore, between the two coaches is the space in which training efforts take place. The standardization of the landscape of modern sport has had an impact on sporting practices and in recent years there has been a desire to neutralize the environment in which sporting competitions take place. [69]

In the case of Stampfl and his athletes, the interval sessions took place on an accurately measured athletics track, whereas Cerutty's athletes often carried out their training around various park circuits that were not standardized. The distinct space of the interval training adopted by Stampfl does not allow for any greater or lesser habit-forming qualities than a non-standardized park trial. Many of Cerutty's weekend training sessions in Portsea involved both *fartlek* around the local golf course and repetitions around the Hall circuit. The size of the oval is immaterial in the sense that the given length of any loop could be used by both Cerutty and his athletes on which to gauge their progress. Indeed it appears that particular loops were adopted as a standard measure. By establishing training based on one-half, one and two times this measure while timing the efforts, Cerutty was able to translate this directly by comparing it to racing results.

In the early 1950s, when John Landy was making a name for himself, the tracks on which he ran in Australia were mostly made of grass. Had he been on a modern cinder track in 1952, when he ran four minutes and two seconds for the mile on a number of occasions, he could have beaten Bannister to the first sub-four minute mile. [70] A standardized 440-yard grass track is by a matter of degrees more 'natural' that the cinder track at Iffley Road or White City, the venues where Bannister raced. This may have been one of the reasons that Cerutty did not worry about the training surface. Cerutty, with his passion for style, no doubt believed the resistance found in more natural surfaces made for better runners. What is interesting is that in a recent interview in which Landy referred to missing out on being the first to break the four-minute barrier he asserted: 'I felt that all I needed to do was run on a better track. . . . the tracks were shocking. They had holes and divots and were uneven.' [71] What is clear is that much of the training engaged in by Landy had much in common with the methods of Stampfl, to the point where during the 1954 season he did numerous time trials. [72]

## Conclusion

The methods of Franz Stampfl and Percy Cerutty may be seen as relying on distinct environments where the habits and dispositions highlighted as socially important in the theories of Bourdieu and Merleau-Ponty can be developed. Neither of the figures so central to the quest for the first sub four-minute mile in the early 1950s has escaped the process of myth-building about their methods. Stampfl has been painted as a figure who relied heavily on the use of the stopwatch and the establishment of structured training programmes, without having lived the experience – a textbook coach with little concern for his athletes. Yet a close reading of Stampfl's belief about coaching highlights a man deeply concerned for the welfare of his athletes, as he was with fine-tuning them in a systematic manner:

> By meeting the athlete, by talking to him on all manner of subjects, by learning something of his background and ambitions, he can form a very accurate understanding of the man and of what makes him tick. Armed with this knowledge, he can prescribe the form of training most likely to produce the best results. [73]

The myth surrounding Cerutty often revolves around his personal philosophy – the creed of the Stotan – which is distinct from the science employed by Stampfl. In comparing the training of Landy [74] and Elliott [75] it is possible to speculate that Cerutty's creed was little more than a publicity stunt to attract fee-paying athletes. [76] Cerutty's methods were only different in terms of the spaces and sites where most training took place, these being, on the whole, less rationalized than those used by Stampfl. [77] Where the training of Landy has been detailed in the build-up to the 1954 season, it highlights a reliance on the stopwatch and specifically time trials. [78] For Elliott however, there is great mystery surrounded the training that he did to achieve a complete career as an unbeaten miler. Perhaps this is not surprising, since Elliott has always celebrated his association with Cerutty, whereas Landy fell out with the eccentric teacher before the 1954 season. Therefore Landy had no reason to keep his training a secret.

To Lydiard, who by the close of the 1950s was beginning to be noticed as a coach of high quality, it was not what coaches advised that was important but how this information was put together:

> All coaches know the different methods of training – fartlek, long steady, striding, sharpening, repetition, sprinting – they all have the parts of the puzzle, but they don't know how to put them together correctly, mainly through lack of practical knowledge of the event. Coaching is more than a science. It is an art, bringing the athlete right on the relevant day. [79]

Suffice to say in the 1950s both Franz Stampfl and Percy Cerutty were able to achieve the right mix and piece together the puzzle by bringing numerous athletes to a peak when it mattered.

## Notes

[1] To mark the 50th anniversary numerous books were published, including J. Bale, *Roger Bannister and the four minute mile* (London, 2004); J. Bryant, *3:59.4: The quest to break the first four-minute mile* (London, 2004), B. Phillips, *3:59.4: The quest for the four-minute mile* (Manchester, 2004).

[2] A recent paper argues against this analysis: see M.G. Phillips and F. Hicks, 'Conflict, tensions and complexities: athletic training in Australia in the 1950s', *International Journal of the History of Sport*, 17 (2000), pp. 206–24. Phillips and Hicks are specifically interested in the cultural environment surrounding coaching in Australia, whereas this current examination's particular focus is on events surrounding the first four-minute mile, when Stampfl was working in the UK.

[3] See P. Bourdieu, *Outline of a theory of practice* (Cambridge, 1977); Bourdieu, *Distinction: A social critique of the judgement of taste* (London, 1984); Bourdieu, *The logic of practice* (Oxford, 1992).

[4] See M. Merleau-Ponty, *Phenomenology of perception* (London, 1962); Merleau-Ponty, *The structure of behaviour* (Pittsburgh, PA, 1963).

[5] M. Foucault, *Discipline and punish: The birth of the prison* (London, 1979). Also, for a Foucaultian analysis of the coaching of Cerutty and Stampfl, see Phillips and Hicks 'Conflict, tensions and complexities', pp. 217–19.

[6] Graeme Kelly, *Mr Controversial: The story of Percy Wells Cerutty* (London, 1964).

[7] Franz Stampfl, *On running* (London, 1955).

[8] For example the reason that Stampfl became such an influential coach was the result of his influence in the running of the first four-minute mile. See R. Bannister, *The first four minutes* (London, 1955) for an account that downplays Stampfl's involvement. Bryant, *3:59.4*, pp. 229–39 suggests otherwise.

[9] Lydiard and G. Gilmour, *Run to the top*, 2nd edn (London, 1967), p. 15.

[10] L.J. Kimayer, 'Reflections on embodiment', in J.M. Wilce, ed., *Social cultural lives of immune systems* (London, 2003), pp. 282–302, 285.

[11] T. Csordas, *Body/meaning/healing*. (London, 2002).

[12] See Bourdieu, *Outline of a theory*; Bourdieu, *Distinction*; Bourdieu, *The logic of practice*; D. Leder, *The absent body* (Chicago, 1990); Merleau-Ponty, *Phenomenology*, Merleau-Ponty, *The structure of behaviour*; Chris Shilling, *The body and social theory* (London, 1993).

[13] G. Ryle, *The concept of mind* (London, 1949).

[14] Merleau-Ponty, *Phenomenology*.

[15] Nick Crossley, *The social body: Habit, identity and desire* (London, 2001), p. 123.

[16] Merleau-Ponty, *Phenomenology*.

[17] Crossley, *The social body*, p. 125.

[18] Merleau-Ponty, *Phenomenology*.
[19] Bourdieu, *Distinction*.
[20] Merleau-Ponty, *The structure of behaviour*.
[21] Stampfl, *On running*, p. 37.
[22] Merleau-Ponty, *The structure of behaviour*.
[23] Bourdieu, *Distinction*; P. Bourdieu, 'Program for the sociology of sport', in S. Kang, J. MacAloon and R. DaMatta, eds., *The Olympics and cultural exchange* (Seoul, 1988); P. Bourdieu, *Sociology in question* (London, 1993).
[24] Andrew Blake, *The body language: The meaning of modern sport* (London, 1996), p. 201.
[25] Adolphe Abrahams, *Fitness for the average man* (London, 1952), p. 25.
[26] Bannister, *The first four minutes*, p. 183.
[27] Roger Bannister, 'Foreword' in Stampfl, *On running*, p. 5.
[28] Bale, *Roger Bannister*, p. 5–9.
[29] Bannister, *The first four minutes*, p. 121.
[30] Stampfl, *On running*, p. 147
[31] Bannister, *The first four Minutes*, p. 121
[32] Chris Chataway, 'Preface' in Stampfl, *On running*, p. 7.
[33] Stampfl, *On running*, p. 147.
[34] Ibid., pp. 43–4, 35–6.
[35] John Bale, *Running cultures: Racing in time and space* (London, 2004), pp. 62–3.
[36] Stampfl, *On running*, p. 47.
[37] Ibid.
[38] Ibid.
[39] Ibid., p. 36.
[40] Ibid.
[41] Kelly, *Mr Controversial*, p. 42.
[42] Ibid, p. 59.
[43] Percy Wells Cerutty, *Sport is my life* (London, 1966). p. 12.
[44] Kelly, *Mr Controversial*, p. 161.
[45] Ibid., p. 54.
[46] Ibid., p. 53.
[47] Phillips and Hicks, 'Conflict, tensions and complexities', p. 211.
[48] See Kelly, *Mr Controversial* and Cerutty, *Sport is my life*. Both of these texts mention his ill health and how he used his study of philosophy and training methods to make himself physically and mentally better, but there is little mention of why he moved to Portsea other than that it was to get back to nature.
[49] Cerutty, *Sport is my life*, pp. 91–2.
[50] Cerutty quoted in Kelly, *Mr Controversial*, p. 55.
[51] Cerutty, *Sport is my life*, pp. 52–61.
[52] Ibid., pp. 55–6.
[53] Kelly, *Mr Controversial*, opposite p. 81.
[54] Fred Wilt, *How they train*, volume 1: *Middle distances*, 2nd edn (Los Altos, CA, 1973), pp. 101–4.
[55] Kelly, *Mr Controversial*, pp. 74–5.
[56] Ibid., p. 75.

[57] Cerutty, *Sport is my life*, p. 39.
[58] Ibid., p. 90.
[59] Kelly, *Mr Controversial*, p. 161.
[60] Cerutty, *Sport is my life*, pp. 90–1.
[61] Stampfl, *On running*, p. 36.
[62] Wilt, *How they train*, pp. 84–8.
[63] Kelly, *Mr Controversial*, p. 160.
[64] Bale, *Roger Bannister*, pp. 89–90.
[65] Ibid., p. 99.
[66] Bannister, *The first four minutes*, plate 33 (opposite p. 192); Bale, *Roger Bannister*, p. 102.
[67] Cerutty, *Sport is my life*, pp. 52–61.
[68] Kelly, *Mr Controversial*, pp. 81–2.
[69] John Bale, *Landscapes of modern sport* (London, 1994), pp.109–10.
[70] Jim Denison, *Bannister and beyond: the mystique of the four-minute mile* (Halcottsville, NY, 2003), p. 22.
[71] Ibid, p. 22.
[72] Wilt, *How they train*, pp. 101–5.
[73] Stampfl, *On running*, p. 38.
[74] Wilt, *How they train*, pp.101–5.
[75] Wilt, *How they train*, pp. 84–8.
[76] Cerutty, *Sport is my life*, p. 35.
[77] Bale, *Landscapes of modern sport*, p. 115.
[78] Wilt, *How they train*, p. 101.
[79] Lydiard and Gilmour, *Run to the top*, p. 15.

# Index